J W POWELL

# We Your People

*Since we are now joined to Christ,*
*we have been given the treasures*
*of redemption by his blood*
*(Ephesians 1:7)*

*Wandering Stream*
*Literary and Publishing*

jimpowell@wanderingstream.org

second printing

COVER ART BY KYLE WILLIAMS
kyle@wendylynn.com

# Table of Contents

## Part one: We Your People

**Part Two: Keys for Unlocking the Golden Scroll**

Other books by the author:

The Ruction
The Revolution

Unlocking the Golden Scroll

# Acknowledgements

There were influencers who shaped and colored the dynamics of this book. They provoked me to reach deeper, speak simply and make better connections with the readers. Their constructive and often provocative observations bridged a message of redemption's treasures to those hungry to discover them.

Liz and Preston Lewis, you guys started the construction of the bridge. I wasn't making the link, and you let me know. That kind of honesty is solid gold to a writer. Liz, thank you for allowing me to receive from your literary training and gifting. Preston, I know you had input with the critical analysis; I so appreciate it. Thank you both for your friendship.

Margaret Cantrell, thanks for applying the final touches on the manuscript and your light to the shadowed areas. A good editor, who can find? Her worth is far above precious jewels.

Penny and Jean Rodgers, thanks for reading the original manuscript and rendering your analysis. Your critique was heard and appreciated.

# Introduction

*"Since we are now joined to Christ, we have been given the treasures of redemption by his blood — the total cancellation of our sins, all because of the cascading riches of his grace. This superabundant grace is already powerfully working in us, releasing within us all forms of wisdom and practical understanding." (Ephesians 1:7-8)*

When I was a kid, treasure hunting was a mystical part of childhood. Creating stories about lost booty was imaginative. Making maps for others to find and following their instructions until discovery was made adventurous.

Treasure hunters pursue historic artifacts, buried stashes and perhaps the noble venture of archeologically validating truth. Whether they seek wealth gained then lost by others through advancing time, calamitous weather, or the demands of war, treasure is their goal. Special detectors explore historic sites and pathways. Deep-diving submarines search for wealth-laden ships lost at sea. It seems pointless that in the end, even treasure hunters leave this world without their treasures.

In another realm, there are world changers with the treasure of God's hand displayed on their lives. These people take destiny, wisdom and practical understanding to heights most minds cannot comprehend. They break open new trends in manufacturing, physics, military advances, politics and ecology; often overcoming long-standing agendas of resistance along the way. In my oft-extensive readings of historic figures, the hand of God had obviously taken the hand of some from birth. He prepared them for difficulties, they being key players for his purposes at specific times. Although Father God will accomplish what he has set his will to do with these people, it would be an eternal loss if these individuals did not put their hand in Jesus' hand to finish their course.[i]

My points are these: Earthly treasures of any size or accomplishment have little value apart from God. The treasures of redemption can never be lost. This rich treasury is gained by asking and believing what God says in his Word and living life by his Spirit. Although the road is narrow and difficult, loving devotion to this purpose is a delight to our heavenly Father.

*The steps of the God pursuing ones follow firmly*
*in the footsteps of the Lord, and God delights in*
*every step they take to follow him. (Psalm 37:23)*

Jesus' most repeated invitation was, "Follow me!" He led people to this invitation in various ways: through his words, through healings and miracles, and through revelation of the Kingdom of God. Regardless of the means used to bring up the subject, his conversations revealed the hearts of people he encountered. Those he engaged would never be the same.

What I seek to explore, in part, is Jesus' challenging invitation — its rewards and its costs. Regardless of where you are on this path of life, what you are about to read will shed light for your feet and reveal the feet of Jesus ahead of you. It will also reveal his heart for you.

We belong to Jesus. What does this belonging mean regarding everyday life? We do not belong to the values of our culture nor the desires of our own ambitions. We belong to God with an identity fully immersed in his nature, shifting us from ordinary people to extraordinary influencers of our surroundings. It's an empowered lifestyle in partnership with heaven which we'll see in the chapters ahead.

God encounters us with his Word to the degree we are fully alive with it. Allow me to make a bold statement. We can become the Word. That's not something you hear frequently. I'm excited to open this treasure for you.[ii]

The Bible is so profound I call it the Golden Scroll, a nickname which began with an adventure novel I wrote. The journey toward this renaming began with my life's verse of the Bible.

> *"Your promises are the source of my bubbling joy;*
> *the revelation of your word thrills me like one who*
> *has discovered hidden treasure." (Psalm 119:162)*

Before The Passion Translation presented a deeper expression of this, there was the New King James Version.

"I rejoice at Your word as one who finds great treasure."

The Golden Scroll is a thrill to unlock. It possesses treasures and unfathomable mysteries of redemption for us to find and activate. Once found and possessed, redemption becomes our relational catalyst with God and our community; the focus of Kingdom advancement.

We Your People is also an in-depth look at God's commitment to reveal himself to everyone on this planet. Starting with you and extending from you, you are the most amazing revelation of Jesus. Through your commitment to follow him, you become a feast for those who hunger for his revelations.

Beginning with 2nd Chronicles 7:14, I present ownership of who we are. God says about us, "My beloved, my children — you are my people." We hear his heart, receive ownership and believe what his cross and resurrection accomplished to bring us to this choice. When we believe in his provision, our hearts

4

respond with, "Our daddy, our friend — we affirm we are your people."

It is my prayer that through these words you will be inspired to envision God, yourself and others differently, and appreciate the life of oneness promised by Jesus in John 14 through 17. When Jesus was in his earthly form he told Philip, ". . . for anyone who has looked at me has seen the Father. . . the Father is living in me and I am living in the Father."

Jesus asked the Father, *"I pray for them all to be joined together as one even as you and I, Father, are joined together as one."*

Being in Christ is the richest of redemption's treasures. How do we take possession of this wealth in this life? We have this potential through our abiding in the Word and the Spirit as completely as Jesus did. We become powerful habitations of heaven, receiving and giving heaven's wealth in partnership with our Father. Wealth such as this awaits us in this life. And in the process, we discover God himself as our Faithful Shield and Abundant Reward.[iii]

There are two parts to this book. Part two, Keys That Unlock the Golden Scroll, is instructional. These short chapters lend canvas, brush and color to help you discover portraits like We Your People in the Word of Truth. With these keys, you will learn to creatively paint scenes of spiritual wealth for yourself and others.

May you not only be enriched through this book but encouraged to pursue God with new passion. Now — let's move on to the fun stuff.

Footnotes:

i  Historic example: Dwight Eisenhauer fought in three wars, learning valuable lessons about leadership, before commanding all Allied forces in WW2. Then he led the United States through the tough years of the beginning of the atomic age. Yet he did not receive Jesus as his savior until the last days of his life.

Contemporary example: Elon Musk has a brilliant mind. He sees what needs to happen and brings change. He's paid the price of hardship to learn important lessons; the price any leader must pay. And yet, at the time of this writing, he has not made a solid public profession of faith.

ii   John 15:5-10

iii   Genesis 15:1

# We Your People

*"Everything we could ever need for life and complete devotion to God has already been deposited in us by his divine power. For all this was lavished upon us through the rich experience of knowing him who has called us by name and invited us to come to him through a glorious manifestation of his goodness."*
*(2 Peter 1:3)*

God knows all things, is everywhere, can create anything he desires and feel every emotion at the same time. In addition, he affords us lavish acceptance and focused attention while ruling as King and Lord of heaven and this considerably smaller expanse called the universe. Do those thoughts stimulate an overload? What can't be experienced is often too much to grasp.

*"For now he towers above all creation, for all things exist through him and for him. And that God made him, pioneer of our salvation, perfect through his sufferings, for this is how he brings many sons*

*and daughters to share in his glory. Jesus, the Holy One, makes us holy. And as sons and daughters, we now belong to his same Father, so he <u>is not ashamed or embarrassed</u> to introduce us to his brothers and sisters." (Hebrews 2:10-11) [emphasis added]*

But God had higher aims than to impress us with what he has and does. What Jesus doesn't have is an ego. And because of his great humility, he has no problem introducing us to his Father — and to the rest of his family.

*For he has said, "I will reveal who you really are to my brothers and sisters, and I will glorify you with praises in the midst of the congregation." (Hebrews 2:12)*

Picture this piece of flash fiction with me:

Papa was sitting alone at what appeared to be a simply created pearl desk. Triple golden bands accented it. One at the top and two at the bottom. The desktop was twelve layers of precious stone placed in a stair-step design. Liquid light flowed away from the desk legs and formed a crystalline floor which appeared to be moving toward the emerald rainbow that framed the open door.

The harmonic sound of happy voices and bare

feet were heard before they were seen. Papa smiled, laid his quill pen into one of the folds of the scroll where he had been writing names, and looked up. As usual, Jesus was the first through the door. He was glowing with delight as he led a cloud of fresh faces looking around, awestruck. Papa had just entered their names in The Lambs Book of Life. Although their bodies were still on earth, this was their moment of spiritual re-birth; a first-time experience of encounter.

Papa simply adored these occasions and immediately belly-laughed. Rising, he ran to greet them. Pulling them off their feet, he hugged each one, gave them kisses and welcomed them to his Kingdom.

Jesus waited until Papa was finished with his endearments and formed the small group in a semi-circle. He met his Father's eyes and the love they shared filled the room. Jesus stood beside each one of the group, an arm encircling them, then moved on as he introduced each of Papa's new children, although Papa already knew who they were. As he did so, Papa laid a big hand on each head, kissed them again and blessed them.

He looked each one in the eye and called them by name and said, "I have known you since the foundations of the earth. From now on, you are welcome to this room anytime."

His delight in loving us enriches our lives with the treasure of knowing who he is. His love and kindness are open arms pulling us to give ourselves to him above all other options. It's an environment where lovers dwell and we overcome all obstacles to obtain more of him, receiving precious wealth in doing so.

Song of Songs is beautifully poetic, describing the divine romance with God and should engage and intrigue all of us. It's fiery and passionate; protective and thoughtful; and yet places demands on our affections. A parable written by Solomon, it characterizes the journey of every longing lover of Jesus.

In our western culture, the atmospheres of lovers take on leanings of sensuality. It's rare in entertainment to see storylines built about people in love with each other whose focused connection is solely the pursuit of each other's heart. But counter-culturally, the nature of biblical covenant love is to remain for a lifetime, sacrifice deeply, build through life's changes, learn from unexpected events, and understand the inner workings of each other. Through it all, intimacy grows to a merged unity.

The nature and depth of his unconditional love is seen at the cross. While we were still lost sinners, Jesus laid down his life for us (Romans 5:8). His love enters our life through sacrifice. The fruits of his sacrifice extend to everyone the free gift of eternal life. When we believe, we agree to receive his gift and a deposit of who he is—the Holy Spirit. From there, our love bonds form embryos of incredible transformations birthed from his Word and Spirit.

He says we should respond to what he's freely given by loving him with all our heart, soul, mind and strength (Mark 12:30). We will spend the rest of our lives peeling back the deepening significance of that tiny word all. Finding all requires the catching of the sly little foxes that hinder our unconditional responses to him.

> *"Let me see your radiant face and hear your sweet voice. How beautiful your eyes of worship and lovely your voice in prayer. You must catch the troubling foxes, those sly foxes that hinder our relationship. For they raid our budding vineyard of love to ruin what I've planted within you.*
>
> *Will you catch them and remove them for me? We will do it together." (Song of Songs 2:14-15)*

Compelling love bonds between God and us stir us to discover more of him and withhold nothing to gain what only he can give. As we hunger for more, we choose to overcome every hinderance to gain other revelations about him.

11

This lover platform is foundational to other ways we encounter him.

## Sons and Daughters

I lost my dad as a six-year-old boy. He passed away while on a fishing trip. I didn't realize it so much growing up without him, but the trauma of it hit hard when I had children. Being a dad without real-life examples left me unprepared for fatherhood.

Later on I discovered I couldn't grasp fatherhood until I captured sonship. It was a long, hard-fought and determined struggle; I passionately wanted to possess this truth. Even when I faltered, my Heavenly Father was faithful and encouraged me. Once I reconciled the nature of God's fatherhood with the identity of my sonship with him, it settled many issues.

First of all, I began to feel like I conclusively belonged in the family. Regardless of how I was treated by other people, the truth of belonging was enduringly established. Familiar patterns of orphan thinking tried many times to cause rejection. But freedom prevailed and Papa could build Kingdom realities on this foundation, the cornerstone of which was the reality of Jesus and what he did to bring us into the family.

My Father's house is the reality of God's love for all people and his desire that none perish without experiencing this love. My Father's business is the purpose of advancing his Kingdom and sharing his vast riches of redemption. As his children, we receive and share his spiritual realities with love, honor and obedience.

## Fathers and Mothers

Fathers and mothers are vital to healthy community. While sons and daughters receive instruction, they progress through training to become devoted life-givers. These are mothers and fathers who birth new life in others. They possess keys to perpetuating the multi-generational purposes of God.

Examples of transformation worked out over the years, they bear witness of Father God's patience, goodness and faithfulness. They also possess their own treasures of redemption gained along the way; gold, silver and precious gems of a new creation.

Fathers and mothers shed light on the path of life ahead; share stories of victory and defeat; affirm the power of Holy Spirit to change things, heal and perform miracles; and show love in the best way they can.

They are the stable catalysts of apartment complexes, neighborhoods and extended communities regardless of faith. God loves the whole of humanity, not just believers. These seasoned saints—and I don't mean old saints—represent the father and mother heart of God. They bring to the family identity and nurture.

### His people

These examples and roles are not unique nor exclusive. May I suggest they are one and the same in purpose, yet exquisitely unique in identity. Who we are—whether at home, in the marketplace, workplace or other spheres of influence—is the showcase of Papa God and the people of God. The fruit we bear for him continues to grow with the spiritual children we leave behind. What treasures we receive of transformation stay with us for eternity.

We are a people becoming; becoming lovers, friends, sons and daughters, fathers and mothers, all family. And from the family treasury, we have the honor of representing the Great Redeemer and bearing the signet of his name.

From this royal family, we affirm to the one who spoke the words that created all of it:

> *"We are your people, called by your great name, identifying as treasures of God's redemption and empowered through transformation to deliver his compassionate love to a lost world. May we grow in the grace of surrendering ourselves to you without reservation."*

# What's This About a Name?

*"To everyone who is victorious, I will let him feast on the hidden manna and give him a shining white stone. And written upon that white stone is inscribed his new name, known only to the one who receives it." (Rev. 2:17)*

*"Then I saw heaven opened, and suddenly a white horse appeared. The name of the one riding it was Faithful and True, and with pure righteousness he judges and rides to battle. He wore many regal crowns, and his eyes were flashing like flames of fire. He had a secret name inscribed on him that's known only to himself." (Rev. 19:11-12)*

A name influences the identity of its bearer. In biblical times, names distinguished both people and places but they weren't mere labels. They had purpose in revealing character, personality and even destiny. Naming is still important in Father's heart today.

Revelation 2:17, as stated above, reveals there is a name waiting for us that is perfectly matched with the outcome of our earthly lives. This promise is an encouragement that our struggles and triumphs have a reward. The completion of our transformation is so precious in Father's eyes as to warrant the reward of a new name. Picture this stone with its name as a treasure deeply meaningful to its receiver. This name would be so profoundly identifying and connecting with Father's heart, it would be too intimate to share with another.

Historically, names also reinforced relationships between existing entities. For example, Pharoah changed Joseph's name to Zaphenath-Paneah; Revealer of Secrets. The name stressed Pharoah's point of contact with Joseph as the one who revealed the secret meaning of his dream. It doubled as a statement of authoritative contract to everyone in Pharoah's court; "You mess with ZP, you messin' with me."

Previous to that, God changed Jacob's name to Israel, meaning one who struggled with God and prevailed. Jacob wrestled with God, his adversaries and his mistakes and afterward received a blessing. Today, this name continues to influence a race of people and those grafted in by the grace of Jesus' redemption.

Have you been walking with Jesus for a while? Can you relate to the wrestling match for transformation? Have you struggled to believe for all you've been promised in God's Word? Jacob and Joseph are two of several identifiers regarding this life we live in Jesus as well as the tenacious confidence we need to possess the treasures of redemption. Never give up; there's a reward and a new name waiting for you. There's a lot at stake.

Through the cross and resurrection Jesus bought access to his name. It's faith in his name and sacrifice and the resulting relationship which guarantees our success. We can't fail. (See Psalm 121)

"But those who embraced him and took hold of his name were given authority to become the children of God!" (John 1:12) To take hold of his name means to believe all that Jesus represents and put into practice what he teaches with the power demonstrated by his example and nature.[i] The result is truly becoming God's child.

The Hebrew word for "take" is marital language about covenant and the vows made by each to live out a lasting union; in this case an eternal union. For the bridegroom, he brings her into his house and promises to cherish, provide, protect and give her his good name. The bride receives his name as her own, identifying with him in unity as one. Proverbs 31 describes her unbridled commitment to make his name honored in the gates of the city by her good works. These are the actions of a wife who has everything she needs to leave a lasting legacy.

God takes our lives with the promise to keep us in shalom shalom.[ii]  Perfect peace, perfect well-being, perfect prosperity, perfect joy; it's all given to honor his good name and show himself strong. We have nothing to worry about, Jesus is a good husband.

A good name is a value nearly lost in modern culture. Several of the last generations suffer from the loss of fatherhood, giving rise to confusion about identity and parental disconnection. Family is a blurred and chaotic portrait.

Yet, names anchor belonging. And a family name anchors security. When that is lost, how can it be restored?

God steps in with his name and an unshakable identity tied completely with him. It can't be lost — ever. Starting from the day we enter into relationship with him, he's rewriting our story to align with his purposes. We are assured through faith his authorship will pull it off perfectly.[iii]

God is good beyond all our understanding and has a good name greater than any other. Actually, the Word shows us he has many good names. The context in Revelation nineteen above links his names with the crowns he wears. His names and crowns are expressions of his nature.

When Scripture says we are called by his name, we are beckoned by the authority of his fatherly nature. There is no father like him. He sent his son to show us the depth of his fatherhood. [iv] He would sacrifice his son—the very essence of himself—to give us access to his parenting.

His desire is that no one perish but come to the knowledge of his redemption. He is constantly at work drawing people to himself; the Good Shephard calling hearts of countless souls away from the abyss of sin's destruction.

Let's take a look at the phrase, "called by My name," the lead-off phrase of 2nd Chronicles 7:14.

Called — a small word with extensive breadth of meaning. There are almost twenty assorted applications in the English dictionary. It is used for specific purposes in sports, theater, idiomatic expressions and assorted simple everyday usage. It would be tiresome reading to compare the various behaviors.

To spare you that unnecessary dreariness, I'll draw within the lines of meanings in the Hebrew bible. Its sketches are far more interesting than English words. It is picturing a divine beckoning (summon, attract, invite, draw near) and inscribing (mark, write, print, carve, engrave). These portray rulership, authority, creativity and purpose and with equal importance, a signature from someone deeply in love with us.

God's love never invalidates, forgets nor disregards who he created us to be.[v] Isaiah quotes Yahweh saying, ". . . Yet I will not forget you. See, I have inscribed you on the palms of my hands."[vi] The word inscribed means chiseled or engraved. Our names are engraved in his palms by ancient nails from the cross. It's an eternal memorial. We are always on his mind and his commitment to us cannot be removed.

Our King is delighted to have his children intimately close. So much so, he takes up residence inside us so we don't have far to go. But on the outside of our lives the world culture offers a constant stream of distraction; purveying goods of false satisfaction.

Our Redeemer bought us from a dark world in which we were never designed to flourish. Striving for a personal identity based on dreams formed in the world's ways shapes an inferior design, limiting our Kingdom effectiveness. Saying yes to his design is significant. Surrendering to everything God has in his heart for us will release us to thrive and dream with God.

One example of that idea is the rich young ruler. (Luke 18:22-30)[vii] A man of substance, his personal righteousness identified with keeping the commandments—and he was right in doing so at the time. But Jesus loved him and exposed that his unspoken identity with wealth kept him from discovering the treasures of a better righteousness.

When Jesus confronted other religious Jews, he challenged their claim of knowing God.[viii] He said, "If you really knew God, you would listen, receive, and respond with faith to his words."[ix] They understood the allegation. The shema;[x] which means to hear, was often repeated as a declaration of their faith. They were hearing and speaking liturgical words without responsive dedication, love and faith. When Jesus called them painted tombs,[xi] they accused him of being crazy for pointing it out.[xii] Their self-righteous hearts couldn't hear what he was saying.

Being a listener is more than turning on a digital device and using the noise for environmental background. Jesus made it plain when he encountered the accuser in the wilderness that we shall not live (sustainably flourish) by bread alone (the needs of our natural life), but by every rhema (divinely inspired) word that proceeds from the mouth of God (our need for spiritual substance).[xiii] We live by everything the Lord speaks. Not only the written Word, but by every conversation he has with us and every word we hear through others who speak for him.

Being called and taking his name, Holy Spirit stirs a life of listening and understanding. Our Heavenly Father is always speaking. Everything in creation[xiv] voices visual and audible expressions of what he says and shows who he is.[xv] He whispers or shouts in circumstances to get our attention; a point made throughout the context of 2 Chronicles chapter 7.

Are we listening? And if we hear, are we receiving the

message? And if we understand the message, are we responding?

Our walk with Jesus faces challenges and we need his nature and power to shepherd us through life. A conversation with God reveals stepping stones. He cares for us with focused attention, guidance and protection. He shares his name with us, which in essence means he delights in sharing all he is with us; as much as we can handle. Through his habitation and his words in us he works transformation to prepare us to handle more.

The fulfillment of our true identity and legacy is becoming like him and one with him. The beginning point of that journey is found in Acts 2:39. "For the promise [of the Holy Spirit] is to you and your children, and to all who are afar off, as many as the Lord our God will call" [emphasis added]. And in 1 Peter 2:9-10, "But you are a chosen generation, a royal priesthood, a holy nation, His own special people, that you may proclaim the praises of him who called you out of darkness into His marvelous light."

It is through his name we get on his path of life. And it's to our unique path of life he calls us by name and leads us on.

> Jesus said, ". . . the sheep recognize the voice of the true Shephard, for he calls his own by name and leads them out [of the sheep pen], for they belong to him. And when he has brought out all his sheep, he walks ahead of them and they will follow him,

*for they are familiar with his voice." (John 10:3-4)*
*[emphasis added]*

Footnotes:

i   From John 1:12 in TPT and accompanying footnote. Clarification added.

ii   Isaiah 26:3

iii   Psalm 37:5
iv   John 14:8-11

v   See Psalm 121

vi   Isaiah 49:15b-16, NKJV

vii   See also Matthew 6:19-21, 19:16-24, Mark 10:17-27

viii   John chapter 8

ix   John 8:47, TPT

x   Deuteronomy 6:4. "Hear O Israel, the Lord our God, the Lord is one." As the Shema developed, it came to include three passages. 6:4-9, 11:13-21 and Numbers 15:37-41.

xi   Matthew 23:27

xii   John 8:48

xiii   Deuteronomy 8:3, Matthew 4;4, Luke 4:4

xiv   Romans 8:20-21

xv   Psalm 50:1, TPT. "The God of gods, the mighty Lord himself has spoken! He shouts out over all the people of the earth in every brilliant sunrise and every beautiful sunset, saying, "Listen to me!"

Read also verses 2 through 6.

Romans 1:20, Psalm 119:64

# Follow Me

*"I alone am the Good Shephard, and I know those whose hearts are mine, for they recognize me and know me, just as my Father knows my heart and I know my Father's heart." (John 10:14-15)*

The disciple's[i] call from the Good Shepherd is an invocation into a growing understanding of being "called by your name." It's a summons to be mentored by Holy Spirit into a lifestyle of knowing the Father's heart, then being trained to represent him and act with him to do what the Father wants done with the resources with which he's empowered and gifted us.

The resonance of that call begins with "follow me." It resounds to include losing our lives for his sake, gaining fruitfulness through faithfulness and possessing the abundant flourishing only Jesus can give. It's a lifestyle surrendered at increasing levels to devotion, selfless love and obedience to

God's voice and purposes. For some, that may sound dreadfully dull. For others, who have taken hold of the surrendered life, those thoughts seem to come as a test of our determination to find the treasure.

Holy Spirit may take years or decades to mold, heal and grow a heart to this level of consecration. While I've watched many quickly progress in fruitful development, my journey has been a slow and narrow road, due to my own shortcomings.

My first step toward Jesus was at the age of twelve when I was baptized for the first time. I was likely told at the time what was expected of me, but I had distractions filtering what I was hearing. As it was, Papa stayed engaged with me and protected me from myself. And he was faithful when I needed some hard knocks to get me listening.

More than thirteen years of wilderness followed my baptism while I remained clueless to my need of him and little aware of God's ways. He knew where my heart was, though, and sent my grandfather (my father's father) to talk with me and pray me through to another level. His sudden death in an automobile accident temporarily stopped the momentum while I foolishly believed the world still had something I needed. In time, it was evident the world I knew was bent on an unloving and destructive agenda.

During those years, God faithfully stayed with me and

answered all my questions and encountered me with his goodness until I fully surrendered to Jesus at the end of the year in 1975. I was twenty-five when that happened.

Thick-headed, slow to get it and respond, I plodded along in spiritual advancement. My strong self-will kept tripping-up my walk with Jesus regularly. I lost golden opportunities and wasted a lot of time. Whatever my broken thinking may have been, the pain of loss and regret inspired me to never give up. My devotion to Jesus grew into a tenacity as strong as my self-will. I determined his life was worth fighting for.

In 2010, God raised the bar; I received a summons from Papa to go deeper. I was unlocking a study on the subject of bondservant, purposed to discover a solid depth on the subject. I found challenging characteristics (such as it could be multi-generational)[ii] and strange mysteries (like having your right ear pierced on a doorpost).[iii]

During this study I felt the Lord standing nearby, waiting for me to finish and give him my attention. When done, I met with Jesus to listen to his heart. His response was to be joined with him in living the very life I had researched. As the implications settled in, anxiety settled in also. My weaker inclinations lean toward distraction and losing track of goals. They were more of a problem at the time than they are today. So, I was concerned that I would fail the Lord over the long haul; understanding that it was not good to vow and not keep it.

He gave me until Yom Kippur to respond to his call—just a few days from then. After that, this time of favor would pass. I wrestled with the issue until late afternoon of Yom Kippur when I surrendered to whatever may come and said yes. God had spoken. I heard with clarity and responded with full comprehension there would be a cost. Where we were headed now would redefine everything I lived for.

Over time, I've come to simply define a bondservant's lifestyle as love that chooses him and obeys his voice over everything else. Looking back, he patiently walked me through fire and wilderness for this treasure gain. I don't want that to sound daunting. But I must be transparent. I had issues to work through.

Can I say I have achieved success on the matter? Honestly, I lose focus on a daily basis and fall into wanting what I want. Even with an awareness of the potential fruit of this calling, it's a challenge to be consistent year after year. Thankfully, not only does grace and mercy follow me, his footsteps lead me. It gives me confidence to know that with his help, I can't fail.

Your journey may be a wandering stream like mine; a process taking you to your destiny through the natural topography of life with its deserts, rivers, canyons and mountains. On occasion, that means exchanging your prairie schooner for a dugout canoe or a camel. Whatever the vehicle, the journey toward becoming his cannot stop.

We are his people for dedicated purposes and go through processes leaving identifying characteristics to represent him. It's like an ambassador plenipotentiary; someone given full power in the name of a head of state to deliver a dynamic message.

We honor him by influencing individuals, neighborhoods and cultural mountains.[iv] We also empower the inheritance of future generations through our families and the families we touch in collaboration with him.[v]

> *"I am the Vine; you are the branches. Whoever lives in Me and I in him bears much [abundant] fruit. However, apart from Me [cut off from vital union with Me] you can do nothing. If a person does not dwell in Me, he is thrown out like a [broken-off] branch, and withers; such branches are gathered up and thrown into the fire, and they are burned. If you live in Me [abide vitally united to Me] and My words remain in you and continue to live in your hearts, ask whatever you will, and it shall be done for you."*
> *(John 17:20-23, Amplified Translation)* [emphasis added]

Following Jesus keeps us in close proximity. We are living expressions of his Word and Spirit. Boldly stated, we are one with Jesus, the Father and the Holy Spirit, being trained through our oneness to have authority, use his name and believe

God will produce fruitful results.

Jesus said something that should be on our radar for serious consideration. In John 17 Jesus was talking with his Father,

> *"Holy Father, I am about to leave this world to return and be with you, but my disciples will remain here. So I ask that by the power of your name, protect each one that you have given me, and watch over them so that they will be united as one, even as we are one. While I was with these that you have given me, I have kept them safe by your name that you have given me." John 8:28-30*

He came, spoke and empowered others to represent his Father. The authority given him by his Father is given to us. That level of representation implies he was also an attentive listener just as we would be in representing him.

Jesus continues, "Your Word is truth! So make them holy by the truth. I have commissioned them to represent me just as you commissioned me to represent you."

Our representation is fruitful through living oneness with him. We follow him and give up our lives in exchange for his. The entry point for this life of love is continual emersion in surrender to Holy Spirit. Being God's child and being filled with the Holy Spirit is a privilege so extraordinary, it surpasses our understanding.

Footnotes:

i  Matthew 9:9, 10:38, 16:24 — Luke 14: 26-27, 33 — John 8:31, 13:35, 15:8

ii  Leviticus 25:46, Exodus 21:3-5.  Forever, including children

iii  Exodus 21:5-6, Deuteronomy 15:15-17. Ears bleed wildly when cut. And blood is a sign of covenant. Perhaps a covenant or reminder of hearing and obeying.

iv  Matthew 28:18-20

v  Proverbs 13:22, 17:6, Malachi 4:6, Luke 1:17

# Humble Yourself

*"Lord God, unlock my heart, unlock my lips, and I will overcome with my joyous praise! For the source of your pleasure is not in my performance or the sacrifices I might offer to you. The fountain of your pleasure is found in the shattered heart before you. You will not despise my tenderness as I humbly bow at your feet.(Psalm 51:15-17)*

Your dictionary describes humility as the virtue of being humble. Let's take a step sideways from the substance of humility and simply listen to humble describe its heart and actions.

My old two-thousand-page dictionary spends a few lines on what humble isn't. I like that, it's helpful. Humility isn't arrogant or prideful. It doesn't pretend to be what it truly is not.

Note that these non-definitions are defining attitudes of self-importance; pride, arrogance and pretention.

Then there's more lines describing what it is. In plainness, it is marked by meekness or modesty in behavior, attitude or spirit, while showing deferential or submissive respect. That is, putting oneself low in rank, quality or station.[i] Having expanded these variables to expose humility's breadth, let's shrink it to capture the present context—bowing at Jesus feet.

Authentic humility as character is spiritually powerful, yet it often develops in crucibles. Crucibles of wrongdoings, misunderstandings of Papa's heart, or those assignments to places we would not volunteer to go.

Humility is often shaped from difficulties created through choices we've made. And if, for some reason, we don't set up these situations for ourselves, he's brilliant to provide opportunities to grow humility for our good.[ii]

Wandering through the short quote from Psalm 51 above is a pathway. It begins with a heart engaged with pleasing God. Then recognizes that our performance and sacrifice do not necessarily mean we are connected at the heart. Discovering our dishonesty is humbling.[iii] We don't work for God, we work with God.

Performance requirements and misplaced sacrifices are

often religious replacements for walking with God in deep communion. Our brokenness feeds the need to perform and sacrifice for someone we hardly know; someone we think is putting demands on us. When we ultimately exhaust ourselves on the alter of self-imposed demands, it can be shattering. The resulting turmoil leads to a broken and humble tenderness.

Through this pathway, our focus returns to the purpose of our existence; communion with God while discovering and sharing his treasures of redemption. Nurturing the active dwelling of Holy Spirit in us and listening for his heart shines light on precious realities of oneness. We begin to discover who we are and how we relate to who he is.

Papa God has a lot of practice with our straying loyalties. When our internal do-er wants more than our be-er is experiencing; when our narrow road of devotion feels slow-moving and unrewarding, surrender is a life-line keeping us connected. Surrender is a core element of humility, that is; making ourselves lower than God, submitting to his leadership and letting go any ownership or control of our life.

Jesus presented it profoundly. "If you truly want to follow me, you should at once completely disown your own life. And you must be willing to share my cross and experience it as your own, as you continually surrender to my ways." (Mark 8:34)

Herein dwells the heart of this chapter; the surrender of our ways for his ways through humility. Surrender implies a conflict needing resolution and cessation. There's a running argument between our flesh and his Spirit; our ways and his ways.

> *"So then, beloved ones, the flesh has no claims on us at all, and we have no further obligation to live in obedience to it. For when you live controlled by the flesh, you are about to die. But if the life of the Spirit puts to death the corrupt ways of the flesh, we then taste his abundant life." (Romans 8:12-13)*

My past has painful reminders of self-important choices I made. Years were wasted foolishly pursuing my own agenda. God has addressed the attitudes, healed the pain, restored the years and taught me to trust him. It is my hope this book will spare you at least some of these misfortunes and set you in a better position to receive. And having received, freely give when and where Jesus leads.

Jesus' ways are better than our ways and always require a first by faith grasp to make it living reality. At the top of the list is the position of sharing his cross. "For if you let your life go [as Jesus did on the cross] for my sake and for the sake of the gospel, you will experience true life." (Mark 8:35, emphasis added)

John Wesley, who spoke a slightly different English in prayer during the 1700s, left us an example of a life made low before God:

> *"I put myself wholly into thy hands: put me to what thou wilt; put me to doing, put me to suffering, let me be employed for thee, or laid aside for thee, exalted for thee, or trodden under foot for thee; let me be full, let me be empty, let me have all things, let me have nothing, I freely, and heartily resign all to thy pleasure and disposal."* [iv]

Detached from this world's distractions, he humbly set his sights on God alone. Like the champions of faith listed in Hebrews chapter eleven, he and those he did life with lived as those who belonged to another realm.[v]

It's true for us as well. When we wholeheartedly humble ourselves and seek God where he is, he will meet us where we are. Since Holy Spirit dwells within us, there isn't far to go. There's little in the way of formula for seeking him and perfection is not required. Jesus simply promised that sustained persistence and overcoming would be rewarded.[vi]

Then we will pray as David did:

> *"Let my passion for life be restored, tasting joy in every breakthrough you bring to me. Hold me close to you with a willing spirit that obeys whatever you say."* (Psalm 51:12)

Footnotes

i   American Heritage Dictionary, fourth edition. Houghton Mifflin Company

ii   Romans 8:28, James 1:2-4

iii   John 15:1-11. Jesus tells us of our need for connection and life-receiving in him.

iv   John Wesley, Directions for Renewing Our Covenant with God, 2nd edition   (London: F. Paramore, at the Foundary, Moorfields, 1781) 13-14

v   Hebrews 11:13, TPT

vi   Matthew 7:7-11, Luke 11:9-10

# And Then, There Is Prayer

*"As for me, because I am innocent I will see
your face until I see you for who you really are.
Then I will awaken with your form and be fully satisfied,
fulfilled in the revelation of your glory in me!"*
*Psalm 17:15*

Biblical prayer has facets and functions and fashions. Not fashions as in clothing, but fashions such as methods. And like humility's variances, exploring them all in this small snapshot of the big picture would unnecessarily dull our focus. But there is a brilliant facet on this gem that is worth looking into.

Solomon's father, King David, set us up to read what he believed. When David was faced with open opposition, he went to prayer. He walked through his circumstances with confidence that God had everything worked out and David was on hand for the occasion.

The Hebrew text of Psalm 109:4 is merely two words; *anni tefilah*, which reveals a unique picture. Literally, it says "I am prayer!" The Passion Translation enlarges it to, "I will pray until I become prayer itself." It portrays prayer as unity with God on an all-encompassing scale; a union which stays with us in every season of life and every hour of the day.

This oneness concept begs a question or two. For one, why aren't we talking about it more dynamically and more frequently? Can we be using different words or saying it another way so as to dull its importance? Does scripture reveal we include a similar experience with the Word? And if so, what about the Spirit?[i] Let's unlock this a little in this chapter and we'll do more throughout the book.

Consider this discussion between Jesus and his disciples.

*"I am the Way, I am the Truth, and I am the Life. No one comes next to [draws near to] the Father <u>except through union with me.</u> To know me is to know my Father, too. And from now on you will realize that you have seen him and experienced him."*

*Philip rejoined, "Lord, show us the Father, and that will be all we need!"*

> *Jesus responded, "Philip, I've been with you all*
> *this time and you still don't know who I am? How*
> *could you ask me to show you the Father, for anyone*
> *who has looked at me has seen the Father. Don't you*
> *believe that the Father is living in me and that I am*
> *living in the Father? Even my words are not my own*
> *but come from my Father, for he lives in me and*
> *performs his miracles of power through me. Believe*
> *that I live as one with my Father and that my Father*
> *lives as one with me — or at least, believe because*
> *of the mighty miracles I have done." (John 14:6-12)*
> [emphasis added]

Jesus revealed his relationship with his Father; they are one. When he is in prayer with his Father in John seventeen, he brings up an identical design about us that is often skimmed over in our spiritual formation.

> *"And I ask not only for these disciples, but also*
> *for all those who will one day believe in me through*
> *their message. I pray for them all to be joined as one*
> *even as You and I, Father, are joined together as one.*
> *I pray for them to become one with us so that the*
> *world will recognize that you sent me. For the glory*
> *you have given me I have given them so that they*
> *will be joined together as one and experience the*
> *same unity that we enjoy." (John 17:21-22)*

Jesus became one of us. Through the cross and resurrection he would activate the love gift of being one with him. What we do with this treasure is a glory of our earthly life.

He gave us spiritual wealth beyond our ability to apprehend and utilize. In this endeavor, we need him to teach us. Through faith, hope and love we engage and sustain our journey toward being one with Jesus. Hunger for deep relationship with God and perseverance keep us going when treasure is being dug out of the barren terrain and tough situations that expose our humanity.

Perhaps intentionally, Jesus made things difficult to grasp so we would dig deeper, question tenaciously and keep after the prize. When he told his disciples they must eat his flesh and drink his blood to have eternal life, many turned away and quit following him.[ii] "Oh my gosh! We have to be cannibals?" For any literalist, it would be the first picture to come to mind.

So it is when we face hard-to-understand difficulties and experiences in our life. We don't see it for what they are intended to do. We may be tempted to walk away or let disappointment kill the passion we have.

I have faced this almost every year of my walk with the Lord. I have to crucify something of my fleshly nature or my passion to possess his nature grows cold.

There is only one solution. Humble myself, turn to him, stand face-to-face, lean in and listen for more of my Father's heart. It's always my choice to stay. As Peter stated, "But Lord, where would we go? No one but you gives us the revelation of eternal life."

When we are fully one, or at least heading toward it, our objectives and pathways will have full light from the one who is light. When we turn from our wicked ways, we will see plainly his brilliant ways before us.

When we draw near to him, he draws near to us.[iii] It is then we find the warmth of our oneness in prayer: a lavish spiritual blessing from the heavenly realm; a love gift from heaven's dazzling treasury.

---

Footnotes:

i  John 14:12-17, 15:7-8, 17:11

ii  John 6:53-65

iii  Hebrews 4:16, 7:25, James 4:8

# Insensitive Seekers

*"Here's the one thing I crave from God, the one thing I seek above all else: I want the privilege of living with him every moment in his house, finding the sweet loveliness of his face, filled with awe, delighting in his glory and grace. I want to live my life so close to himthat he takes pleasure in my every prayer." (Psalm 27:4)*

Hear the hunger in David's voice. Do you catch the intensity of key words: crave, privilege, sweetness, delight and pleasure? Feel the tug of a heart convinced only one thing will satisfy.

Love empowers passionate seeking. Desperation empowers relentless seeking. Repentance empowers humble seeking. Seeking God has tunnel vision. When seeking is purposeful, intentional and singular in pursuit of a connection with God, everything of less importance will be met with what looks to others like insensitivity. In other words, what appears to be perceived urgency in our earthly lives must wait. Whether seeking to appeal for help, right standing or just enjoying his company, his presence sets order and purpose.

New Covenant believers haven't far to go for his presence. He's inside us and with us all the time. He never leaves us. There are no exceptions with the word never even though our feelings may try to deceive us. In his presence we safely open our hearts, being honestly vulnerable and stilling our fears. Practice instills confidence our seeking will be rewarded.

*"I will pray until I become prayer itself."*[i]

David was a seeker. Better said, he was a zealous and strong-willed pursuer for the heart of Yahweh. The psalmist's lyrics are evidence of whole-hearted determination to see God in his battles, his mistakes, his legacy and most importantly, his own heart. He's still encouraging us through song with examples of how God met his challenges. David was after connection with God.

What does God use to draw you to him?

Correction and training are daily ingredients of intimacy with Father God. If we neglect or ignore these instructive times, we find ourselves ill-equipped to hold steady to the prophetic course of Kingdom advancement. We cannot just do as we please.

*"My child, don't underestimate the value of the discipline and training of the Lord, or get depressed when he has to correct you. For the training of your life is the evidence of his faithful love. And when he draws you to himself, it proves you are his delightful child." (Hebrews 12:5-6)*

As a busy monarch, David faced constant harassment from political schemes. Invisible crosswinds designed to oppose his leadership had to be frequent. Resistance and distractions left him needing prayerful navigation. Civil, political and military matters placed drama on his mind and demands on his time. With issues falling through the cracks at the end of the day, compulsive decisions for easy solutions would have been tempting. Neglecting to seek God would have put him in wrong places at wrong times with the wrong attitudes. Scripture is filled with this scenario.[ii]

Is it possible for us to fall prey to the same snares? We all face similar situations in part or in full. Choosing presumptive easy-path relief in desperate circumstances can leave us in consequences we are stuck with for years. I speak from experience.

Seeking the Lord's heart allows him to train us for wisdom, timing and strategy with situations appearing to be chaotic.

Love and trust produce patience to let him work reconciliation, restoration and hope to relationships.

Another example: a road block is thrown in front of us to reveal we're going the wrong direction. Time to seek him. When our pathway has strayed, he lights an onramp back to the path of life.

Let's say we've been on a long path of obedience in the same direction. The grind of the pathway has drained us of joy and excitement. We need refreshing. Time to seek him.

Resources have dried up; a strong indicator of something needing attention. We've encountered a financial famine. Time to turn, face God, ask questions and listen.

Having a financial need is not necessarily an indication we have strayed. Waiting on God—a close cousin to seeking—can be a synchronizing time to ensure all aspects of our life move forward together. In the long term, it strengthens our confidence when people, provision and the release to take action align supernaturally. Later, we can look back and see God's hand in what took place.

Does God Play Hide and Seek?

*"Ask, and the gift is yours. Seek and you'll discover. Knock, and the door will be opened for you.*

*Every persistent seeker will discover what he longs
for. And everyone who knocks persistently will one
day find an open door." (Matthew 7:7)*

Connection with God is a persistent lifestyle. Creating
quiet moments for listening, seeking, asking, knocking and the
pursuit of Kingdom life is a commitment to seek God until he is
found. Often, a quick response from God stops our pursuit of a
complete answer. Our resolve to reach deeper is satisfied with
the first response. Father knows when we are ready for all of the
counsel in his heart.  It's in those times he appears to be hiding.

Does love turn away all options and choose a progressive
life of surrender?[iii]

*"Love the Lord Yahweh, your God, with every
passion of your heart, with all the energy of your
being, with every thought that is within you, and
with all your strength." (Mark 12:30)*

Footnotes:

i  Psalm 109:4b  Literal Hebrew says, "I am prayer."

ii  Joshua chapter 9 for instance

iii  Matthew 10:39, 16:24, Mark 8:34,
    Luke 9:23, 14:33, 17:33, John 17:10

# Turns, Turns, and More Turns

*"When people turn to you, they discover how easy you are to please — so faithful and true! Joyfully you teach them the proper path, even when they go astray. (Psalm 25:8)*

The most important turn any of us make is turning to God. By turning, I mean we determine to get in his presence and find his heart. Whether the first time or forty-first time, we need to turn aside from one thing or another and face him.

Life is seasonal, with seasons of easy turns and hard turns, major turns and small turns, safe turns and risky turns. Sometimes unexpected turns throw confusion at the navigation of our seasons. These are opportunities to turn and be taught.

Turns force us to ask questions, "Where am we going?" or, "How did we get here?" and "What did we do to deserve this screwball twist of fate?" My most often cry is, "There's got to be more than this!" It may not sound like a question, but it is at the core.

Pathways of circumstance cross paths of choice. Desperate, we may be tempted to grab an easy solution. This becomes an around the mountain again solution which doesn't endure and we end up where we started.

On the other hand, a well-reasoned choice without full input and clarity from Father God may leave us in a place we aren't meant to be. This doesn't mean those places are inherently bad. It could be as simple as choosing something we desire instead of waiting for God's best. And because of it, we aren't thriving. We may justify the lesser fruit of it and settle for what we're getting. But frustration will provoke us to pursue a more durable solution.

On yet another hand, something inside us isn't working right and we have no way of stopping the dysfunction. Holy Spirit is bringing part of our broken soul to our awareness for healing and freedom. Why would he do that? Let's explore a short rabbit trail.

Papa wants deep-reaching, unshared time with us. The torah gives three appointed times during the year (Passover, Pentecost, and The Feast of Tabernacles) when his children quit what they were doing and turned to present themselves before

Yahweh.[i] It didn't matter what they were doing, it was time for a face-to-face with God. Today, as sons and daughters of his Kingdom, these appointed times are solid invitations to his court for something different than our daily experiences.

Holy Spirit prepares us for encounters with him. Often uncomfortable to our inner being, Holy Spirit purifies us for presentation before the King. Jesus tells us, *"What bliss you experience when your heart is pure! For then your eyes will open to see more and more of God."* His presence reveals what is yet to be purified in us. And when we submit to his purification, God reveals more of his presence. It's a beautiful cycle.

There is a true story about Smith Wigglesworth and eleven others having a prayer encounter with God in New Zealand. They were in a room together praying when the presence of God started to increase. As Wigglesworth prayed another person observed, *". . . as strange as it may seem, the Exodus began* (one by one they began to leave the room). *A Divine influence began to fill the place. The room became holy. The power of God began to feel like a heavy weight. With set chin, and a definite decision not to budge, the only other one* (other than Wigglesworth) *now left in the room hung on and hung on, until the pressure became too great, and he could stay no longer. With the flood gate of his soul pouring out a stream of tears, and with uncontrollable sobbing he had to get out or die; and a man who knew God as few do was left alone immersed in an atmosphere that few men would breathe in."* [ii]

Although nothing remotely resembling the power-filled experience written above, I had a similar experience. Holy Spirit wanted access to a part of my heart that was blocked with a wounded self-will. His presence increased until I felt I would lose all sanity. It was weighty and crushing. When I surrendered and let him have what I was holding on to I was freed to enter his presence.

We all have similar limits. The word tells us that no one has seen God and lived. Our fleshly nature cannot live in the fullness of his light. We can grow closer through increasing commitment to living by the Spirit.[iii]

There is good purpose in the transformational processes of our journey. Papa delights in revealing more of himself and letting us experience his presence. But his presence can be more light than we can bear, starkly revealing where our broken fleshly nature is hindering his closeness. He won't give us treasures we are not prepared to fight for and keep.

> "You must catch the troubling foxes, those sly foxes that hinder our relationship. For they raid our budding vineyard of love to ruin what I've planted within you. Will you catch them and remove them for me? We will do it together." (Song of Songs 2:15)

Often our way needs intervention and restoration. It's at these times he reveals our foxes of complacency, unbelief and predispositions of concern for the cares of this life and gives us the choice to catch them and send them on their way.

Jesus wants us to turn and pursue him, the ultimate solution. He delights in our rescue and is always willing to show us the path of his choosing.[iv] A path where his footsteps lead us, where his voice is clear and intimacy points to the primary purpose of our existence—himself.

He provides a spiritual roundabout to exit wicked ways (more on this in the next chapter) and enter the high way of heavenly living.

> *"Arise my love, my beautiful companion, and run with me to the higher place. For now is the time to arise and come away with me. For you are my dove, hidden in the split-open rock. It was I who took you and hid you high in the secret stairway of the sky. Let me see your radiant face and hear your sweet voice. How beautiful your eyes of worship and lovely your voice in prayer." (Song of Songs 2:13-14)*

Do you hear his acceptance and affection, his focused attention with you? He protectively hides you in secret places where no one else will detract his attention from you. When he's with you—you are exclusively his. What is more, he put Holy Spirit within you for the same purpose; to give you a secret place where he has the only key to the door.

*"So I kneel humbly in awe before the Father of our Lord Jesus, the Messiah, the perfect Father of every father and child in heaven and on the earth. And I pray that he would unveil within you the unlimited riches of his glory and favor until super-natural power floods your innermost being with his divine might and explosive power.*

*"Then, by constantly using your faith, the life of Christ will be released deep inside you, and the resting place of his love will become the very source and root of your life." (Ephesians 3:14-17)*

The greater grace of his full access to us breaks open the full power of a heaven to earth reality. The Word made flesh in us becomes a dynamic spiritual influence changing the world around us.

*"Break open your Word within me until reve-lation-light shines out! Those with open hearts are given insight into your plans." (Psalm 119:130)*

Self-control and faithfulness are fruits of his presence. It is not only the ability to say no to bad things. It is also the ability to say yes to something so completely good all other options are eliminated. When that good thing is or becomes highly valued, we turn from what we are doing and pursue that which is valued to the exclusion of everything else; even good things.[v]

By the Spirit we become people who turn toward him and listen, then receive and respond with faith to what he says. [vi] Since he always has something on his heart and because he enjoys sharing those thoughts with us,[vii] the intention of his voice is endearing, inviting, revelatory or corrective. He wants us prepared for Kingdom success being ambassadors of his will.

As we move into the greatest harvest and its accompanying power ever seen in our generation, the call of heaven to embrace our unique purposes and labor together for its success is loud. Our lives, time, energy and other resources belong to Jesus.

We have turns to make. Only by following in his footsteps will we make wise and discerning turns. Turns to be made with heaven and earth in mind. Turns in the natural and the spiritual realms.

> *"As for us, we have all of these great witnesses who encircle us like clouds. So we must let go of every wound that has pierced us and the sin we so easily fall into. Then we will be able to run life's marathon race with passion and determination, for the path has been already marked out before us.*
>
> *We look away from the natural realm and we fasten our gaze onto Jesus who birthed faith within us and who leads us forward into faith's perfection."* *(Hebrews 12:1-2)*

Footnotes:

i  Deuteronomy 16:16

ii  Harry V Roberts, New Zealnad's Greatest Revival (by an eye witness) Aukland, New Zealand: The Pelorus Press Ltd, 1951

iii  John 3:6, 6:63, Romans 8:1-13, Galatians 5:16-17, 6:8

iv  Several Psalms address his rescue / deliver heart for us when we call to him and even when we can't see our need.

v  Something like this syayement may have originated with Bill Johnson.

vi  John 8:47

vii  Read Song of Songs (also called the Song of Solomon) to grasp his heart toward us. I highly recommend The Passion Translation for this. It powerfully reveals Jesus' love for his bride.

# What in the World is a Wicked Way?

*"If My people who are called by My name will humble themselves, and pray and seek My face, and turn from their wicked ways, . . ." (2 Chronicles 7:14, NKJV)*

*"Search me, O God, and know my heart; Try me, and know my anxieties; And see if there is any wicked way within me, And lead me in the way everlasting." (Psalm 139:23-24, NKJV)*

Ask three people what wicked means and you'll likely get four opinions. Why? Wicked is not on the lips of contemporary conversations. So, venturing a definition from the average person on the streets would likely be inviting a guess based on personal experience. Will the average person talk about truly evil wicked? Or will they offer up the malicious wicked of sociopolitical opposition? Maybe it's slang-speak for something considered cool.

The original Hebrew gives more than ten words translated as wicked throughout the Old Testament, all with different shades of meaning. For literary honesty and clarity, the scriptures above reflect the same English usage, but originate from dissimilar Hebraic sources (*ra* and *eseb*).[i]

With that in mind, wicked may not be what we think. And if so, what turn from which wicked way is Papa God looking for from us? A journey through only relevant shades pertaining to our life in Jesus will make the answer to that question clear.

The wicked way of 2 Chronicles 7:14 pertains to what is not morally pure or good. It's the same word used in Genesis regarding the tree of the knowledge of good *and evil*. It is also used to describe the condition of the people of Sodom. The larger Hebraic picture portrays a wickedness which severs relationship and causes trouble, misery and distress. Over time, the face communicates what is growing in the heart—anger, loathing, bitterness, sorrow and anxiety—signs of disconnect from God.

The wicked ways of Psalm 139 are actions and attitudes caused by mistaken views (we could just call them lies) which lead to physical, emotional and spiritual suffering. They lead to the toilsomeness of unrelenting self-effort or mental anguish derived from unfavorable circumstances. They can also lead to our heart's misalignment with God, reflected in words spoken to loved ones and friends. Then there are communications that are critical, harsh, unduly blunt and a constant flow of negativity. Believing lies produces interactions which are hard to give and hard to receive.

I remember the years and seasons of peeling back layers of lies I believed—the misshapen views of my Father and his love for me. I was unable to understand my brokenness. I couldn't find vulnerable trust that allowed God to have access to my heart. My blindness of unbelief hammered my life with unrelenting self-effort to overcome failure and unfavorable circumstances. What successes I experienced were short-lived. I understood little of my partnership with Jesus which would enable me to steward opportunities and use them as stepping stones of progress.

But when healing brought the courage to trust, his blessings were lavish. He could trust me with Kingdom treasures. And I could trust him to be kind and patient while I learned to use them fruitfully.

When Papa blesses us, he uses these blessings to set us up for success; success that is not the by-product of self-sufficiency. Spiritual success is evidence of our wholeness with God and his people. Just to be clear, success is laying hold of the treasures of redemption and stewarding their wealth for God's purposes. It may include an abundance of financial resources, but that is not the defining measure of spiritual wealth and maturity.

Another level of personal breakthroughs started when I learned the amazing value of surrender, a form of turning to God. Psalm 139:23-24 lays out a platform for understanding what happened in my heart.

> *"God, I invite your searching gaze into my heart. Examine me through and through; find out everything that may be hidden within me. Put me to the test and sift through all my anxious cares. See if there is any path of pain I'm walking on, and lead me back to your glorious, everlasting ways — the path that brings me back to you."*

Although nothing is hidden from God, I can choose to not deal with what's in my heart. It's a leaning I caught from Adam when he was still in the garden. And like Adam, I must acknowledge my brokenness, quit trying to fix myself with my own understanding and let his Word and Spirit transform my inner man. Never, at any time, has God said to have faith in myself. I need faith in God and accept his provision of grace for abundant life.

As I learned to surrender hidden things and let him in, I grew to trust his love and believe his purposes are always good. I still remember the line I crossed when I chose to take the next step and invite him to have access to my hidden stuff. This included whatever I was blind to, hidden issues I was unaware of. As freedom from the path of pain came, Papa taught me to guard and keep this new treasure by speaking truth to the lies that were the familiar thinking processes of my former broken-ness.[ii]

Until we overcome our doubt and unbelief, lies prevent us from keeping our advances toward our promises. Herein is a nugget of wisdom and a picture of God's training. He will give us a partial fulfillment of a promise knowing we will lose it to our immaturity. It exposes what is still needing inner work. When the transformation is advanced sufficiently. He returns the promise. And through the training we go again until we possess the promise permanently.

When God's people crossed Jordan into the promised land, their entry was by a miracle—the water stood still upstream. But taking possession of their inheritance was won by obedience to God's voice and battles with the squatters preventing access to the promises. At times they helped each other, needed correc-tion and sang songs for deliverance and victory.

Overcoming wicked ways opens our hearts to possessing the miraculous promises God has for us. One of those ever-lasting ways is letting God have control of our lives. Surrender acknowledges we are striving for control and breaks the need to control.

Let's take an etymological[iii] journey through the history of control.

The origins of the word *wicked* is Anglo-Saxon, the earliest recorded form of English. Wicca described a sorcerer. Moving forward to Middle English, wicche described a witch. Witchcraft and sorcery imply the use of power to control human destiny. Controlling our own life outside of partnership with God through witchcraft using words and stubbornness to force getting what we want falls under this pattern.[iv]

While Satan seeks to destroy our destiny with human toil and self-reliance, God seeks our well-being with faith-tested surrender to his control, where we live and move and have our being wrapped fully in the love of God.

> *"Make God the utmost delight and pleasure of your life and he will provide for you what you desire the most. Give God the right to direct your life, and as you trust him along the way you'll find he pulled it off perfectly." (Psalm 37:4-5)*

Unbelief and anxiety are wicked ways. Worry prevents the fulfillment of the purposes of God. Taken from the annals of personal struggles, when I faced lack, I had fear. My journey from desperation to find faith came through wave after wave of lack. Every wave pushed me closer to the freedom of faith; learning to trust my Father for everything.

Desperation will cause us to make wrong choices. Faith will patiently wait for the right solution. There is nothing like the lessons of provision to teach us about the affects of anxiety. It's a victory that helps us find everlasting ways and enjoy the life of peace, hope and love.

When surrounded by a world that considers us sheep to be slaughtered—seducing anyone who will listen into its ways—we will come face-to-face with what hasn't been transformed inside. It's not always obvious until we are faced with strong resistance. Will we be safe during these times? Of course, because God is gracious to keep us and instruct us. But his purpose is to make us more than victorious, he builds us to be conquerors.[v]

With God's help we will be solid in proclaiming, as David did, *"Listen to my testimony, I cried to God in my distress and he answered me. He freed me from all my fears!" (Psalm 34:4)*

Without fear, we walk in the everlasting ways of the Kingdom of heaven. From our heavenly position we use faith, hope, love and the knowledge of spiritual realities to see heaven enacted and empowered on earth for the purposes of God.

For one purpose, we are filled with Holy Spirit to become like him, becoming a new creation. From that living expression of a changed life, we are infused with and reveal the nature of Jesus.

For another purpose, we are filled with Holy Spirit to demonstrate to others the riches of God's kindness, that everyone may hear, with anointing, the words we speak and see by the works we do, the treasures of his redemption and be reconciled to God.[vii]

Footnotes:

i  2 Chron. 7:14 is Strong's #H7451: ra. Psalm 139:24 is Strong's #H6089: eseb

ii  Proverbs 4:23

iii  Etymology is the study of the origin of words and the way in which their meanings have changed throughout history.

iv  1 Samuel 15:23. "For rebellion is as the sin of witchcraft and stubborness as is as iniquity and idolatry." (NKJV)

v  Romans 8:35-37

vi  Acts 1:8

vii  2 Corinthians 5:18-20, Colossians 1:21

# God Hears from Heaven?

*". . . then I will hear from heaven, and forgive their
sin and heal their land."*

This is Yahweh's grace-filled response to Solomon's prayer,
"And may You hear the supplications of Your servant and of
Your people, Israel, when they pray toward this place. Hear
from heaven Your dwelling place, and when You hear, forgive."[i]

It isn't difficult to comprehend the exchange. Yahweh
has received the dedication of his recently completed temple.
To Solomon, it represented a significant earthly connection
between God and man.

Why would God need to hear from heaven? He is heaven
and present everywhere as well. But Solomon understood the
request, and so did God. I'm the one who read it differently than
intended. What it meant was, I will hear *you* from *my place* in
heaven.

In Solomon's day, heaven and earth needed a connection.

God and humanity still needed a connection. Building the temple was representative of covenant man moving toward God to gain reunion. But the blood of sacrificial animals could not fulfill a lasting reunification.

The day would come when humankind's inner world would be restored to the original design of completed fellowship. The treasures of redemption would become spiritual realities.

In the very beginning—in the genesis of creation—Elohim (the composite counsel of the Godhead) decreed to *"make man in our image,"* put breath in his lungs and an inner spirit to respond to God.[ii]

Unfortunately for us all, the serpent deceived the man and the woman. And they traded God's image for an image of their own making. Without God's leadership, humankind was set on a trail of darkness and death.

Before the creation of the earth, Yahweh had seen this failure and made provision for Adam's redemption. He would send his own son and give him life through the image of man.

> *"One man's disobedience opened the door for all humanity to become sinners. So also one man's obedience opened the door for many to be made perfectly right with God and acceptable to him." (Romans 5:19)*

The coming Emanuel; God with us, our Messiah; would live amongst us and be heaven; telling us everything he heard. Then by his death and resurrection, he would forgive all our sins, heal our disconnection from Father's presence, take up residence in these human temples and shape his likeness in us.

This abiding place gave us a return trail of light and authority to be God's eternal children. Like the original Garden of Eden, we would always be in God's presence and be given the message of redemption with power to take it into all the world.

It was understood in Old Covenant thinking, heaven was beyond reach of the ordinary person.[iii] Today, ordinary people who believe in Jesus as Lord and Savior and receive the Holy Spirit, have access to heaven. We are seated in heavenly places with every spiritual blessing lavished upon us.[iv] We become extraordinary people in co-habitation with heaven.

*"If there is a physical body, there is also a spiritual body. For it is written: The first man, Adam, became a living soul. The last Adam became the life-giving Spirit. However, the spiritual didn't come first. The natural precedes the spiritual. The first man was from the dust of the earth; the second Man is the Lord Jehovah, from the realm of heaven. The first one, made from dust, has a race of people just like him, who are also made from dust. The One sent from heaven has a race of heavenly people who are*

*just like him. Once we carried the likeness of the man of dust, but now let us carry the likeness of the Man of heaven." (1 Corinthians 15:44-49)*

Equipped with his likeness, we are set on a journey to understand spiritual realities, hear from heaven and receive the generosity of its wisdom to deal with the spirit realm.ᵛ We become the people we were destined and designed to be.

In that sense, we are prophetic people. By definition we ascribe to the treasure of hearing from God before we speak or do. By definition, the Hebrew word shema implies we are listening to receive what he speaks and the revelations from what he has written. It's the life of being a people who cherish our treasures and respond in obedience to his voice..

We have heard from heaven through the voice of Jesus. Heaven came to us and spoke the words of eternal life. And having heard, we believed.

*"And what is God's "living message"? It is the revelation of faith for salvation which is the message that we preach. For if you publicly declare with your mouth that Jesus is Lord and believe in your heart that God raised him from the dead, you will experience salvation." (Romans 10:9-10)*

This redemptive treasure of salvation begins its brilliance with the golden grace of forgiveness.

Footnotes:

i  2 Chronicles 7:14 and 6:21, NKJV

ii  Genesis 1:26-31

iii  Psalm 36:5, 57:10, 108:4, 144:7

iv  Ephesians 1:3, 2:6

v  James 1:5

# Forgiveness Fixes Everything

*"Our faith in Jesus transfers God's righteousness to us and he now declares us flawless in his eyes. This means we can now enjoy true and lasting peace with God, all because of what our Lord Jesus, the Anointed One, has done for us. Our faith guarantees us permanent access into this marvelous kindness that has given us a perfect relationship with God. What incredible joy bursts forth within us as we keep on celebrating our hope of experiencing God's glory." (Romans 5:1-2)*

The blood sacrifice of Jesus on the cross and his resurrection three days later guarantees unconditional forgiveness of sins and permanent access to his kindness. With little exception, every sin and transgression—past, present and future—is blotted out of our history with God.[i] Believing God regarding this loving provision is the birth of a life that was dead because of sin. It is our redemption.

This radical forgiveness also reveals his passion to reconcile[ii] and restore.[iii] This marvel of generosity will be a source of awe and mystery into eternity.[iv] While on earth, it's his motivation for binding up our wounds of brokenness, freeing us from captive thinking, comforting our sorrow and creating beauty where there was failure.[v] Isaiah 61:9 says, because of what he does for us, we will be known as mighty oaks of righteousness. Jesus, the Tree of Life, multiplies himself in us so we become trees of righteousness.[vi]

David says, "By the strength of his forgiveness his anger does not break out in judgement."[vii] A solid walk with God knows the freedom we have to dive with confidence into the deep waters of God's forgiveness.

*"For You, Lord, are good, and ready to forgive,*
*and abundant in mercy to all those who call upon*
*You." (Psalm 86:5, NKJV)*

Papa God created an unforgettable experience so I would never forget the character of his forgiveness. I don't remember the backstory for the incident. It was in regard to one of my many failings. When I asked him to forgive, he yelled in my ear, "It's done!" The time between my request and his response was a nanosecond. The intensity of God's response moved the atmosphere around me.

When I asked why he did that, he said, "I want you to know

how quick I am to forgive and get you back on the path of life."
As this father-son conversation went on, I understood how
important it is to receive his forgiveness and get on with life
quickly. Choosing to hang out with blame, shame and guilt will
cause unnecessary interruptions in his life-flow.

> *"Yet he was the one who carried our sicknesses
> and endured the torment of our sufferings. We
> viewed him as one who was being punished for
> something he himself had done, as one who was
> struck down by God and brought low. But it was
> because of our rebellious deeds that he was pierced
> and because of our sin that he was crushed. He
> endured the punishment that made us completely
> whole, and in his wounding we found our healing."*
> *(Isaiah 53:4-5)*

We are not partners of guilt, blame and shame or ambassadors of crime and punishment thinking. Jesus suffered on
our behalf so we could demonstrate his love and our freedom.
The Kingdom of God is right standing with God, peace and joy
and freedom thinking. He set us free not only for our benefit,
but also for the benefit of his Kingdom. It is impossible to move
forward in transformation and advance his Kingdom chained to
the heavy ball of condemnation.

> *"So now the case is closed. There remains no accusing
> voice of condemnation against those who are joined in*

*life-union with Jesus, the Anointed One." (Romans 8:1)*

When teaching his disciples about community life, he showed forgiveness as a necessary constant for keeping their hearts healthy. Peter asked how often he should forgive his brother.[viii] Jesus implied it should be done whenever the brother asked, up to four hundred and ninety times. I'm sure impatient Peter was not happy with this answer. It's human nature to punish those who wrong us with retribution or disconnected relationship. Jesus put an end to that with their dialogue.

When love discovers the unconditional nature of God running through it, our personal demonstration will move toward greater capacity. When we experience the consistency of our Father's care for us, our revelation of the wealth we carry comes alive and spills over toward others. And because we are often in need of healthy relationships, we need forgiveness spilling over on us too.

The Greek word for saved [sozo] not only describes our rescue from darkness, it includes our being brought into health and wholeness.[ix] Our healing of body, soul and spirit is meant to set us up for mutual success in doing life with those around us.

All this is our redemption. It begins with forgiveness and is fully realized in forgiveness. Our transformation, and the messes we make in its processes is sustained in forgiveness. Through the forgiveness and removal of our sin our inheritance is shaped from its beginning.

> *"And since we are his true children, we qualify*
> *to share all his treasures, for indeed, we are heirs*
> *of God himself. And since we are joined to Christ,*
> *we also inherit all that he is and all that he has".*
> *(Romans 7:17)*

Footnotes:

i  One thing could affect this promise — if we do not forgive transgressions against us, God will not forgive our transgressions (Matthew 6:12-15) Another one must be pointed out because Jesus said it in Matthew 12:31-32. Words said against the Holy Spirit will not be forgiven.

ii  Reconcile defined: 1. To reestablish a close relationship between (two or more people), to become friendly or peaceable again, 2. To settle or resolve (like a dispute), 3. To bring (oneself) to accept or be resigned to something not desired, 4. To make (two apparently conflicting things) compatible, harmonious or consistent

iii  Restore defined: 1. To bring back to an original or normal condition. 2. Reestablish existence or use. 3. Repair or fix.

iv  1 Peter 1:12

v  Isaiah 61:1-9

vi  From Brian Simmons' footnotes in Isaiah 61. The Passion Translation

# Heal the Land, Heal the Promise, Heal the Blessings

*"For God is satisfied to have all his fullness dwelling in Christ. And by the blood of his cross, everything in heaven and earth is brought back to himself — back to its original intent, restored to innocence again! Even though you were once distant from him, living in the shadows of your evil thoughts and actions, he reconnected you back to himself." (Colossians 1:19-21)*

After we have humbled ourselves and turned to Father God and sought him, prayed and found forgiveness, another process in our journey begins. Reconciliation,[i] restoration and rejuvenation[ii] are always on Papa's heart. His makeover resumes so we can get back on the path of abundant life.

When the Bible speaks of land, it alludes to visible and invisible substance.

Visibly, the whole earth is the Lord's. Whatever allotment of Kingdom real estate God gives for our stewardship, we hold as caretakers of his possession. That can be as humble as a tent in an urban wilderness or as noble as a country vineyard. We aren't going to take our dirt with us when we step into our eternal inheritance. It is left here as our handed-down material legacy. What we own or do not own in this life will be tools to shape our character before then and perhaps the character of our progeny.

Invisibly, land signifies characteristics of inheritance, promise, influence, spiritual legacy and fulfillment. Fruitfulness of these life-realities are not necessarily measured on whether or not we own land; although God may use it to influence that end. Our personal fruit will be as active and measurable to the degree our hearts are knit together with Jesus.[iv] Without his partnership, our harvest is diminished; we will thrive in our collaboration with him.

Several scholars agree that the mention of land or earth[v] in scripture points to both literal and figurative applications. Brian Simmons, principal translator of The Passion Translation, translates Psalm 37:11, *"The humble in heart will inherit every promise"* — figurative. The New American Standard Bible says, *"The humble will inherit the land"* — literal.

A. T. Robertson, a New Testament scholar of the early twentieth century, refers to the land as representing promise.[vi]

My wife and I spent a few months in Israel at our Father's invitation. We learned that the land of Israel is important to our Father, so it became important to us. Being there opened our understanding about God, the significance of the land of Israel and its sustained relationship to his people; both Christians and Jews. Jeremiah 7:12 states that his name abides there. I have a satellite picture of Israel that shows what appears to be the Hebrew for Yahweh etched in the topography.

So much begins in the land and continues into God's plan for the whole world. Our legacy of faith comes from Abraham. His sojourn to, in and around the Promised Land showed us his trials and victories, messes and imperfections. What land he purchased was but a taste of what was promised. He believed God, though, and exampled for us the pathway of increasing faith.

Abraham's obedience to offer Isaac as a sacrifice played out on the same mountain as Father God's sacrifice of his son Jesus on the cross. The experiences that tested Abraham's love also gave us insight about Yahweh's love. In like fashion, our personal trials and sacrifices will test our love for him while revealing more depth of his love for us.

The years of Joshua's leadership of taking ownership of the Promised Land, with its conflicts for tribal inheritance and personal legacies, were fought as examples for us to see our lives in confrontational context. Their enemies had to be displaced and defeated for full possession to be a reality.

*"From the moment John* [the baptizer] *stepped onto the scene until now, the realm of heaven's kingdom is bursting forth, and passionate people have taken hold of its power." (Matthew 11:12)* [emphasis added]

Actively seeking heaven's kingdom is the pursuit of a treasure contended against by the world; and at times, our own broken soul. One of the battlefields for that treasure is our resolve.

J R R Tolkien stated he did not write Lord of the Rings to be a Christian allegory. But nuggets of his biblical beliefs leaked onto the pages. The story of the dwarf kings and the Kingdom under the Mountain is a case in point. The dwarf king's lust for earthly treasure distracted him from healthy rulership of the dwarf kingdom. His obsession with wealth led to the breakdown of alliances and eventually the defeat of Erebor, the dwarf fortress.

A considerable time later, the Hobbit, Bilbo Baggins, stumbled on the vast treasure of dwarf accumulation lost to the dragon, Smaug. Not only did Bilbo discover the treasure, he encountered the dragon committed to preventing access to the wealth and whose purpose was to kill hope related to claiming it as an inheritance. After a courageous and tense exchange, Smaug stated to Bilbo, "There is something you carry made of gold, but far more precious." The ring, symbolic of covenant, wrapped around his finger, allowed him to maneuver through the dangerous traps of the dragon and plunder a powerful piece of authority, the treasured Arkenstone. The ring represents the character of perseverance and the faith benefit of being hidden in Christ.

Today's Israeli has a unique courage and boldness to take possession of their land, even when the odds are against them. Their war is an "in your face" daily reality. The enemy is always near, throwing flaming darts (missiles) into the thick of their hope and future. To not be ready for battle is costly. So, they stand as examples of perseverance.

Personal battles which shape our character may delay or hinder possessing our land of promise while we are learning to fight for breakthrough.[vii] Resistance of doubt or unbelief, squandered opportunities and unforeseen obstacles, defer our hope of promise fulfilled. Yet these very battles form the resolve to keep every part we eventually possess.

> *"We all experience times of testing, which is normal for every human being. But God will be faithful to you. He will screen and filter the severity, nature, and timing of every test or trial you face so that you can bear it. And each test is an opportunity to trust him more, for along with every trial God has provided for you a way of escape that will bring you*

*out of it victoriously." (1 Corinthians 10:13)*

Our battles are controlled times of training. Scripture says that God never gives us more than we can handle. I know that's not what it feels like when personal losses and difficult circumstances are stretching us beyond our breaking points.[viii]

I know I'm not alone when the scream of my heart was, "I can't take any more!" and it gets worse. Sound familiar? I look back now with head shaking and think, "That was just boot camp."

Although these tests get messy and we crumple under the strain, we need to understand we have not failed. The process is building endurance and capacity for greater exploits. There will always be greater battles to face. Have you ever wondered why God gives us small things first?

That doesn't mean thoughts of inadequacy go away. Lies are part of the enemy's weaponry. Accusation aimed at our insecurities seek to break our resolve and wear down our passion. It's through training that we learn to use truth and perseverance to gain our victories. In learning to fight to win, we have to take a few punches. God's training prepares us for success and greater authority, never failure.

*"Now you [the seventy] understand that I have*
*imparted to you all my authority to trample over*

*his [Satan's] kingdom. You will trample upon every demon before you and overcome every power Satan possesses. Absolutely nothing will be able to harm you as you walk in this authority." (Luke 10:18-19)* [emphasis added]

Our enemy is bent on destroying anything good. Each generation impacts the legacy-scape. One generation can fall prey to Satan's scheme and leave a subsequent generation with social and spiritual obstacles. When we get saved, Jesus covers our personal past. But there are occasions when Holy Spirit reveals a certain family event that has left an obstacle to the advancement of the Kingdom in successive generations. In those revelations there needs to be a reconciliation of the books in heaven to heal the generational breach. (See 2 Samuel 21:1-14)

While we may not understand why generational issues come up, I certainly don't, our obedience as Kingdom priests to make intercession is important. The land, the promises and the blessings belong to our Father. And he gives them to us for our stewardship. As we are faithful to take possession, he gives us increase.

*"Celebrate with praises the God and Father of our Lord Jesus Christ, who has shown us his extravagant mercy. For his fountain of mercy has given us a new life — we are reborn to experience a living,*

*energetic hope through the resurrection of Jesus
Christ from the dead. We are reborn into a perfect
inheritance that can never perish, never be defiled,
and never diminish. It is promised and preserved in
the heavenly realm for you." (1 Peter 1:3-4)*

2 Peter 1:2-4 adds that we have *magnificent* and *precious*
promises through which we are partakers of Jesus' divine
nature.

The Kingdom of God is filled with treasures unsurpassed by
the corrupt values of the world. Faith, understanding, self-control, patient endurance, godliness, mercy and unending love
form in us because Father sees us surrounded in Christ.[ix] These
values make us unstoppable.

I may have said before, and if so, it's worth repeating; the
revelation of the Word of God and the unlocking of its spiritual
realities is treasure of untold worth.[x] The values of this world
distract us from our pursuit of heaven's treasure — God himself.
And he rewards the faith of those who pour all their passion and
strength into keeping him.[xi]

Jesus told us to store up for ourselves treasures in heaven.[xii]
The Greek words for storing up and treasure have the same root.
It is the word from which we derive thesaurus, a treasury book
of words.[xiii] In essence, Jesus is saying to treasure our treasure.
If we treasure the promises God speaks into our lives, whether

from the Word of God or prophetic words given expressly for us, it is beneficial to review and guard them. If we have neglected these promises, it is time to turn and seek reconciliation and restoration.

The Word of God is similar. We may know the Word well, even memorize it. But when we believe the Word, it becomes activated and alive, penetrating to our core of our soul and spirit. It interprets and reveals the true thoughts and secret motives of our heart. It takes us out of hiding and puts us before God.[xiv] When we love Papa, opening our heart to him is not as scary as it may seem. He is gracious and merciful and waits until we are ready to hear.

Believing the word has profound and exciting challenges. Ask yourself about things you read in the Gospels and Letters.[xv] "What would my life look like if I truly believed and acted upon this Word?"

> *"Every spiritual blessing in the heavenly realm has been lavished upon us as a love gift from our wonderful heavenly Father, the Father of our Lord Jesus — all because he sees us wrapped into Christ. This is why we celebrate him with all our hearts."*
> *(Ephesians 1:3)*

There are extraordinary blessings we have yet to tap into as the body of Christ, blessings we are not ready for. They are too weighty for our current spiritual condition. That will change as we mature as his spotless bride.

> *"Through our union with Christ we too have been claimed by God as his own inheritance. Before we were even born, he gave us our destiny; that we would fulfill the plan of God who always accomplishes every purpose and plan in his heart."*

> *"Now we have been stamped with the seal of the promised Holy Spirit. He is given to us like an engagement ring is given to a bride, as the first installment of what's coming! He is our hope-promise of a future inheritance which seals us until we have all of redemption's promises and experience complete freedom — all for the supreme glory and honor of God!" (Ephesians 1:11, 12a, 13b-14)*

There's something about a love willing to forsake all that releases greater grace. When our hearts are whole and healed, we will love wholeheartedly and embrace the greater levels of love available to us. When we are bonded deeply, we will follow Jesus anywhere. According to Romans 8:31, *"If God has determined to stand with us, tell me, who then could ever stand against us?"*

I could put the entirety of Romans 8 here to set up our equipping and understanding of what we are being prepared for. A season is coming when the spirit of this world will be set against God's people, and we will be prepared.

> *"For nothing in the universe has the power to diminish his love toward us. Trouble, pressures, and problems are unable to come between us and heaven's love. What about persecutions, deprivations, dangers, and death threats? No, for they are all impotent to hinder omnipotent love, even though it is written:*

> *All day long we face death threats for your sake, God. We are considered to be nothing more than sheep to be slaughtered!"*

> *Yet even in the midst of these things, we triumph over them all, for God has made us to be more than conquerors, and his demonstrated love is our glorious victory over everything! (Romans 8:32-37)*

Perhaps this chapter has taken an unexpected pathway. I hope it has helped us to empty our hands and hearts of any of this world's material stuff. It's worthless in comparison to the treasures Papa shares with his heirs. Although Heaven's Kingdom realm. Therefore, we hold them loosely.

As Christians, God's greatest glory and triumph revealed through us may be our detachment and our commitment of carrying nothing but his Spirit and authority to love the world around us.

He sent out his twelve disciples with a message: "Heaven's kingdom realm is accessible, close enough to touch." A method: travel light, trust God for everything, bring healing, and deliverance, and raise the dead. A mission: "Freely you have received the power of the kingdom, so freely release it to others."[xvi]

In like manner he sent the seventy disciples with a message: "God's kingdom has arrived and is now within your reach!" It was a mission to go recruit harvesters for the harvest. A method: don't take anything, don't get distracted from Jesus' purpose. Their authority was the same as the twelve.[xvii]

As for you, hear Jesus on this: *"The person who follows me in faith, believing in me, will do the same mighty miracles that I do — even greater miracles than these because I go to be with my Father!"[xviii]*

Footnotes:

i  Reconcile defined: reunite, make compatible, cause to sit happily with, resolve differences.

ii  Rejuvenate defined: refresh, reawaken, put new heart / new life into, reorganize, do makeover.

iv  John 15

v  Hebrew: eretz, Strong's #776h, land, earth, soil, world, region, country.

vi  "Word Pictures in the New Testament," Volume 1, (Matthew 5:5) first published in 1930

vii  See the books of Joshua, Samuel, Kings and Chronicles

viii  2 Corinthians 1:8-11

ix  Ephesians 1:3

x  Psalm 119:8, 11, 20, 33, 55-56, 64, 81-82, 86, 89, 96, 97-99, 130, 133, 140, 152, 162, 169. The Passion Translation

xi  Hebrews 11:6

xii  Matthew 6:19-21

xiii  A book of synonyms, often including related and contrasting words and antonyms.

xiv  Hebrews 4:12-13

xv  I left out the Old Testament for a reason. This is not the place to address "torah observance" nor address what in the Old Testament came through the cross changed and what ended. It would be distracting from the point of this book.

xvi  Matthew 10:1

xvii  Luke 10:1-9, 17-24

xviii  John 14:12

# Now Where is God Taking Us?

*"Now my eyes will be open and my ears attentive to prayer made in this place. For now I have chosen and sanctified [set apart] this house, that My name may be there forever; and My eyes [my attention] and My heart [my concern] will be there perpetually." (2 Chronicles 7:15-16, NKJV)*

After we've done our bit making renewal of our covenant with God. Repentance is healing the halting steps that kept our walk with Jesus on the byways. Our attentive listening to Holy Spirit has resumed and our roving heart is quieted before the Father, assuring ourselves we will live for his presence. Once again, life is reconciled to its creator. Family life is thriving and smiles glow all around the room while hugs cap off the atmosphere. Now what?

Now is the marking of God's sequential logic, closing out the past and sending it to its place of forgotten nonexistence. He has chosen not to remember what we've done or where we've strayed.

For us it's forgetting all of the past and fastening our hearts on walking the path of life with Jesus, filled with hope.[i] Reconciled — resynchronized to the now.

> *"And now, dear children, remain in him, so that when he is revealed we may have joyful confidence and not be ashamed when we stand before him at his appearing. If you know that he is righteous, you may be sure that everyone who lives in righteousness has been divinely fathered by him. Look with wonder at the depth of the Father's marvelous love that he has lavished on us and made us his very own beloved children." (1 John 2:28 – 3:1)*

An important moment is at hand. We have returned because of his creative stirrings and restored to the expanding enormity of his Kingdom advancement. We've left the false doing thing behind where not being good enough provoked us to live out what we think we ought to be. We've re-entered a realm of unique design where we display his love, kindness and creative genius.

Understand, we haven't returned to simply "going to church." Our journey reaches much further. We engage in intimate partnership with our Father, taking possession of his vast treasure of redemption. Through his wealth we build and advance his Kingdom, his people and the social constructs we influence.

What we've come to, being enfolded in the family of God, are those we will do life with and share the Spirit of perfect acceptance—our full measure of adoption. In conjunction with the adoption process is the growing revelation of God's father-hood. There is no heavenly family without heavenly parents— Father, Son and Holy Spirit. Through this relationship, Jesus lives his life in us![ii] For what end?

> *"Now it's time to be made new by every revela-*
> *tion that's been given to you. And to be transformed*
> *as the glorious Christ-within as your new life and*
> *live in union with him! For God has re-created you*
> *all over again in his perfect righteousness, and you*
> *now belong to him in the realm of true holiness."*
> *(Ephesians 4:23-24)*

When we agree[iii] to belong to God as his people, we accept a multifaceted journey of becoming fully his and letting his new-creation dynamics get formed within. Belonging to Jesus puts us on the highway of holiness leading us to the mountains and valleys of transformation.

Holiness needs a rabbit trail, a word picture and perhaps a synonym or two, to clarify for us ordinary people what we do not use in our daily conversations. For the most part, it is the realm of our inner life, a rich realm we share with Jesus.

Moreover, the Hebrew and Greek verb forms define holiness as dedication, faithfulness and loyalty to God. It places God in a cherished position of honor given no other where Holy Spirit works his master craftsmanship of change.

And while I'm here, a whimsical rabbit trail to the rabbit trail could be beneficial. What do change, transfiguration and transformation have in common? In the Greek scriptures the root word is the same, from which we use the English word, metamorphosis.[iv]

With the help of the rabbits, it is easier to see holiness as our devotion to abiding as one with Jesus (see John chapter 17). It serves as an atmosphere of passion for God's best creativity, changing us into a powerful likeness of Jesus for his purposes. Scripture is clear that our transformation is not only to make us powerful people, but to free us to be sent where powerful people are needed. Embracing the process honors him with our trust. Obedience honors him with our love. Lasting fruit honors him with the reward of his sacrifice.

Jesus will never leave us or forsake us.[v] The Hebraic picture for leave is 'left without power' or 'left feeble'. Forsake expands to 'permanently abandoned, rejected and left behind'. Encouraged with a promise that goes back to Deuteronomy, we should feel comforted. But our comfort zone does not include that he won't ask hard things of us. Remember, Joshua was told more than once to remain very strong and courageous. He was leading people into promise and prosperity. The people of Israel were to conquer and occupy. There would be resistance and the risks would be high.[vi] But the ancient promises given Abraham were to be realized — now. This was the appointed time, no turning back.

It is our love for Jesus that empowers our perseverance when the cost of his discipleship carries a decisive weight. And it seems we may pay the price time and again, only to be confronted with another occasion to choose between flesh and Spirit. Those occurrences challenge us to reach deeper for something greater; surrendering our need for the temporal so we may possess the eternal.

It is fascinating to understand that we often do not know what we are saying yes to until we have said yes. Isn't that the nature of faith? We want to read the fine print of disclaimers and assurances first. But God says, "Trust me!" Our assurance is God alone. He is our adventure of faith. Knowing more about him and following him fills our quest to be like him.

When Jesus said, "Follow me," it was a clear now moment for the one who heard. Any words of hesitation received a rebuke from Jesus.[vii] When we choose to follow God without question,[viii] we are choosing powerful expressions of Kingdom relationship as sons and daughters, as friends and bondservants. All are ambassadors of the Great King.

We often do — and I am no different — We often hesitate and weigh the consequences against what we have now. Surrender is daunting. Whatever our dreams and wherever we are going, our lives will not be the same from this moment forward. Rest assured, it will not.

> *"Let me make this clear: A single grain of wheat will never be more than a single grain of wheat unless it drops into the ground and dies. Because then it sprouts and produces a great harvest of wheat — all because one grain dies.*

> *"The person who loves his life and pampers himself will miss true life! But the one who detaches his life from this world and abandons himself to me, will find true life and enjoy it forever! If you want to be my disciple, follow me and you will go where I am going. And if you truly follow me as my disciple, the Father will shower his favor upon your life." (John 12:24-26)*

Surrender is taking the seed of our life and planting it in the good soil of devotion to Jesus. The promise is our lives will grow in favor from our Father.

Footnotes:

i  Philippians 3:13

ii  Romans 8:10, Colossians 1:27, 2 Corinthians 13:5.

iii  Agreement = amen

iv  Matthew 17:2, Mark 9:2, Romans 12:2, 2 Corinthians 3:18. Metamorphoomai: to change the essential form or nature of something (from Strong's #G3339 and other reference tools)

v  Deut. 31 6-8, Joshua 1:5, Hebrews 13:5.

vi  Joshua 1:1-9

vii  Matthew 8:21-22, Luke 9:57-62

viii  Psalm 89:30-33, Song of Songs 2:15,

# What Are You Growing?

*"For we did not receive the spirit of this world system but the Spirit of God, so that we might come to understand and experience all that grace has lavished upon us. And we articulate these realities with the words imparted to us by the Spirit and not with the words taught by human wisdom. We join together Spirit-revealed truths with Spirit-revealed words. Someone living on an entirely human level rejects the revelations of God's Spirit, for they make no sense to him. He can't understand the revelations of the Spirit because they are only discovered by the illumination of the Spirit. Those who live in the Spirit are able to carefully evaluate all things, and they are subject to the scrutiny of no one but God. For "Who has ever intimately known the mind of the Lord Yahweh well enough to become his counselor?" Christ has, and we possess Christ's perceptions. (1 Corinthians 2:12-16)*

Growing in oneness with Jesus, the crown jewel amongst our treasure-trove of redemption is a process. Discovering the depth of grace and love of Jesus and the Father is an unfolding revelation of what we can be.

Jesus tells us much about the abiding place where the Word and the Spirit are empowered from heaven. Often, when we find these dwelling places, we discover they are in seed or surrender form. Unpacking or growing these spiritual blessings are challenging and rewarding.

All truth comes in seed form. Growing the Word of God into healthy living takes faithful practice and intentionality. Husbandry is agricultural skill in knowing how to grow heathy and strong produce, flowers or other living plants. Considered an art form, good farmers have deep connection with the land, the soil, the seeds, the plants and their productivity.

Husbandry also lends insight for how life, truth and spiritual realities become powerful. An illustration will help you understand what God does when we ask for more—a spiritual lesson from the natural order. If we want an olive tree, Papa gives us an olive. Why?

When given an olive, it must be cared for with the respect and honor it deserves. Unpacking its specific character qualities on a master gardener level takes patience and tenacity and intuitive listening.

The best seeds are prepared from living olives fresh from the tree. The flesh is hammered until tender, then stripped away. The seed is then scrubbed, cleansed and left in water to soak. When the seed is properly prepared, it germinates and has the potential of becoming a strong tree giving oil from its fruit or the varietal flavors of a cured olive; the reward of good husbandry.

Here's an example closer to home.

In family circles our children come to us in seed form. A knowledgeable and spiritual husband and father sees into the life of each person given to his care. No two children will be raised with the same tools. Their inner workings are uniquely different. The husbandry of wives and children can be a book on its own. But the point being made pertains to spiritual connectedness with the family.

Consistently sowing the good seed through intimacy with Jesus is the beginning of a deeper spiritual life. Evan Roberts was strongly instrumental in the Welch revival of 1904-05. He spent much of his life sowing a personal history with God. He learned to live in the secret place in God and cultivate God's presence in his life.[i] His devotion to simplicity was rewarded richly.

Jesus' model of seed and soil shaped my personal goals to dream with God and commit to what is important to him. It's a lifestyle staying connected at his heart and accountable to his design for my life and calling. It's about watching for when good seed comes and ensuring my heart is in fertile condition.

Listening and responding is a large part of the process and consistency is a key. We won't pull it off perfectly. We're still broken, and a work in progress toward being like Jesus while our Father is delightfully and graciously engaged with us in our journey.

What the heavenly voice echoed through the sky about Jesus, he says about us. "This is my dearly loved Son, the constant focus of my delight." It is my hope you will hear God's heart and receive, "You are my dearly loved child, the constant focus of my delight." Apprehending this will change what it means to be his disciple and it will empower what we do and why we do it for him.

In John chapter seventeen, Jesus gave an account of what his Father sent him to accomplish. A list of six items checked off his finished mission. He set the pattern of leading by service and sacrifice motivated by love. And now it was time to pass the baton to his disciples and those who would be his children through them.

His six-item list contains no-shame reminders of our progress and goals which move us forward with a hunger for more. May they be helpful to you in forming your lifestyle and design.

Your intimate time alone with God as well as in corporate settings amongst the body of Christ will shape specifics.

- "I have glorified you on the earth by faithfully doing everything you've told me to do."

- "I have manifested who you really are and I have revealed you to the men and women that you gave to me to reach."

- "Now they know that everything I have is a gift from you."[ii]

- "The very words you gave me to speak I have passed on to them."[iii]

- "Those whom you have sent me to are convinced that I have come from your presence, and they fully believed that you sent me to represent you."

- "Your glory is revealed through my surrendered life."[iv]

There is another gleaned from verse six for us to ask. Have we fastened God's Word firmly to our hearts? The verb picture from the Greek is to continuously watch over in order to protect. The noun picture is to have custody. Possessing the Word deeply will keep us on course for what we are becoming.

We are uniquely crafted by Father's hands. These points are not a measure of performance or success. They are a revelation of what the Holy Spirit can do through our lives and provoke us to ask for more. Spiritual momentum during the journey will draw us toward a deeper life with God.

When passionate for the things and ways of God, impatience can be a major frustration. The principles of integrity, faithfulness[v] and training[vi] must be learned along the way or the fruit of a deeper life and the resulting God-given assignments will not remain.

Relationships have germination processes needing cultivation. Relationships with other believers are eternal. How we relate with them to keep them healthy are shapers of our character. Being aware this statement looks like an aside to the flow of what I've been saying, I'm compelled to say healthy relationships are holistically essential to everything eternal.

Jesus included this understanding as one of the two foundations of the law. Love the Lord your God with all your heart, all you mind and all your strength. and love your neighbor as yourself. We already spent time pondering the prospect of becoming prayer, becoming the Word and becoming the Spirit. More important than those is becoming love. Loving God with every passion of our hearts, all the energy of our being and every thought within us so we are free to love ourselves and those close to us.

We will spend the duration of our lives learning to become

love and discovering the depths of all. One of the difficulties in the process is guarding our hearts from making comparisons about the difference between what we are today and what that little word all looks like.

Our grasp of the depths of lavish grace extended for the processes of our journey cannot be overstated. God's grace is extravagant, recklessly immoderate, showered on us in what appears to be wasteful abundance. It's all designed to keep us moving forward in pursuit of God's high calling as children of the King; a calling of royalty and priesthood.

I was stunned when a British friend stated, "You Americans do not understand the difference between nobility and royalty at all. There's a huge difference!" In the process of seeking to understand, I was enlightened. With my current half-baked American grasp of the subject, I give you this. In British culture, nobles are a privileged class holding honorary titles which can become hereditary. Royals are the family members of the monarchy (king or queen) or in the family line of those who once were sovereign rulers.

While much could be gleaned from this metaphor, my focus is about our belonging in the royal family and being co-rulers with our sovereign God.

Whatever process he takes us through to prepare us for our place in his Kingdom is lavishly wrapped with mercy, grace and love. According to John 14, we are being trained to be as powerfully effective as he was by bringing heaven to earth. He surprises us with adding that we will do greater works than he did. We understand that it is still Jesus doing the works. He has choosen us to co-labor with him.

Will we step up in response and choose what he has for us?

Footnotes:

i  Page 168. Defining Moments, God-Encounters with Ordinary People Who Changed the World, by Bill Johnson and Jennifer Miskov, 2016, Whitaker House

ii  James 1:17

iii Matthew 12:33-37

iv  These six points are formed from John 17:4,6-8, 10, Romans 12:1-2

v Luke 16:10, "The one who manages the little he has been given with faithfulness and integrity will be promoted and trusted with greater responsibilities."

vi  Proverbs 20:27-30, 22:6, 2 Timothy 2:15, 3:16-17

# An Inconclusive Conclusion

Within the wonder, awe and nature of God, dwell his unique communication skills. He can speak a single sentence and give us thoughts taking years to unpack their significance; shades of what he said gaining clarity and substance over time. Great intelligence has little weight for understanding Heavenly revelations and gaining practical wisdom. He often uses people who give themselves to prayer to proclaim what is on his mind. And above all else, Father loves connecting everyone who chooses to be his child.

Our spiritual wealth is hidden in Jesus like treasure waiting to be discovered — heaven's wisdom and endless riches of revelation knowledge.[i] With that understanding, this message to you draws to a conclusion. Yet, it is incomplete because the message of our relationship with Jesus is inspired and illustrated through countless means. What I have written is a mere portion of them.

From the prayer conversation between Solomon and Yahweh in 2 Chronicles 7, we discovered treasures of redemption focused on our consecration to Jesus, unlocked his nature and unlocked our identity and purpose. We had a taste of why that is important.

We are a new creation in process of being fashioned into his likeness; reconciled to his original design. We carry this confidence because of our union with him.

Figuratively, the Holy Spirit makes us living parts of his body,[ii] living stones in a spiritual house,[iii] living letters written by the Spirit of the Living God.[iv] Choosing to be a living part of Jesus makes us powerful.[v] To this depth we agree with the King of kings that "We are your people."

As God's people we can be sons and daughters, kings and priests, friends and bondservants, apostles, prophets, pastors, teachers, evangelists, saints and assorted intercessors. We cannot be all things to everyone as he is. Our design is family living interdependently, united in Jesus to encourage, serve and love one another. And together we deliver his message of faith, hope and love to our communities. His mission is to pour out his Spirit on all flesh. God builds his people through transformation, awakening, reforming and refreshing to equip and commission us as catalysts for that purpose.

He desires that we know him, his nature and his power intimately. Why? Daniel 11:32 tells us. "The people who know their God shall prove themselves strong and shall stand firm and do exploits (for God)." [Amplified Bible] That strength and those exploits, motivated by knowing God as I have shown throughout this book, can be focused at any sphere of influence or task in life. Being a wise parent, a thoughtful neighbor, a fine craftsman, an articulate musician, a sensitive educator and even a politician are arenas for our best to shine with Holy Spirit in partnership.

Father God's mission to advance his Kingdom and build strong people is resisted by enemies of the cross. The resulting engagement initiates conflict. If we find ourselves put in spiritual battles it is because we have been trained to win.

Paul told Timothy as Paul was approaching the end of his life, "I have fought an excellent fight. I have finished my full course and I've kept my heart full of faith. There's a crown of righteousness waiting in heaven for me, and I know that my Lord will reward me on his day of righteous judgement. And this crown is not only waiting for me, but for all who love and long for his unveiling."

It is my hope you have been creatively stirred to study and become the Word. God's Golden Scroll imparts wisdom to experience eternal life through the faith of Jesus, the Anointed one.

Every scripture has been written by the Holy Spirit, the breath of God. It will empower, instruct and correct, giving you strength to walk illuminated paths of godliness. Then you will be God's servant, fully mature and perfectly prepared to fulfill any assignment he gives you.[vi]

An additional focus of this book is illuminating a path for returning to Jesus, to place him as the centerpiece of life. From that point of return, the Word has encouragement to re-engage with him.

*Listen my radiant one —*

*if you ever lose sight of me,*

*just follow in my footsteps where I lead my lovers.*

*Come with your burdens and cares.*

*Come to the place near the sanctuary of my shepherds.*

*My dearest one,*

*let me tell you how I see you —*

*you are so thrilling to me.*

*To gaze upon you is like looking*

*at one of Pharoah's finest horses —*

*a strong, regal steed pulling his royal chariot.*

*Your tender cheeks are aglow —*

*your earrings and gem-laden necklaces*

*set them ablaze.*

*We will enhance your beauty,*

*encircling you with our golden reigns of love.*

*You will be marked with our redeeming grace.[vii]*

Jesus welcomes us always and delights in every step we take to follow him.[viii] From the first step to the last, we are his people. Nothing stands in the way of receiving that identity.

Footnotes:

i  Colossians 2:3

ii  1 Corinthians 12:18-20

iii  1 Peter 2:4-5, John 14:23

iv  2 Corinthians 3:3

v  John 15:1-8

vi Taken from 2 Timothy 4:15-17

vii  Song of Songs 1:8-11

viii  Psalm 37:23

# PART 2

# KEYS FOR

# UNLOCKING THE

# GOLDEN SCROLL

*"Your promises are the source of my bubbling joy;*
*the revelation of your word thrills me*
*like one who has discovered hidden treasure."*

*"Lord, listen to my prayer. It's like a sacrifice I bring to you;*
*I must have more revelation of your word!"*
*Psalm 119:162 & 169*

# Why?

All who believe in Jesus as our Lord and Savior have purposeful journeys with his living Word in front of them. Given the grace for a long life, we will experience various seasons. For instance, my first season had phases of reading cover-to-cover. My brain and heart needed a lot of rich resource to change the way I saw things. So my first years were filled with intense washing out of the old self by the Word and putting in a newly created self through its renewing of my mind.

The next phases slowed to ten chapters a day, followed by a three-chapter-a-day plan that read between the covers in one year. In addition, when I bought a cassette player for my old '63 Ford pickup, I added listening to the Word. Reading and listening to the Bible was one of my two best tools. The other was the Holy Spirit. They were basic seasons and served their purpose to fasten the Word firmly within.

Yet with all the reading and listening, I found it hard to memorize blocks of Scripture. I tried highly recommended memorization systems. But I couldn't stop the memory drain; not then and not now. But Father had something else in mind.

While in bible college, one of my professors introduced my wife and I to discovery study concepts while equipping us to lead small groups at the church we attended. This equipping group was my trail-head to the path of a treasure hunter. Having received these tools, I determined to learn them well and find more.

I have kept some, shed some and gathered others while I learned what works for my thinking processes. Over time, I no longer have to think about them. They're simply there; like the dexterity of muscle memory.

One of my novels; Unlocking the Golden Scroll; is a message which creatively presents the concepts I use in story form. But I knew when I wrote that book, a more serious approach would be inevitable.

The objective of Part Two is to present essential tools to help you see scripture as living pictures and experience the Father and Jesus through Holy Spirit's illumination of their nature. I invite you to explore these tools, learn to use them and find your own treasury of redemption. Exercise these concepts and light up your path of relationships with God and man brilliantly. The pursuit will increase your spiritual health and wealth.

There is more revelation about God, his Word and his Kingdom remaining to be unlocked and shared than an army of scholars can comprehend in one lifetime. With so much to possess, process, build on and grow in, there is no reason for any of us to stop walking in Jesus' footsteps.

My life verse from Psalm 119 is fuel for my study engine. "Your promises are the source of my bubbling joy; the revelation of your word thrills me like one who has discovered hidden treasure." (verse 162)

So, how does one become a treasure hunter of the Word? Let the seeds of what I give you germinate and grow. By consistent and persistent practice, these tools will fulfill your hunger and create a harvest of understanding. Like any tool, usage and opportunity creates mastery.

And having found treasure, further searching gains more reward. Like mining, there are gold nuggets close to the surface. Yet there are veins of gold for those willing to dig. As you find the gold, it is my prayer that you will become the gold.

# Keys for Unlocking the Golden Scroll

*Write the following to the messenger of the congregation in Philadelphia, for the solemn words of the Holy One, the true one, who has David's key, who opens doors that none can shut and closes doors none can open: . . ." (Revelation 3:7)*

Being in God's presence enhances everything we do as well as who we are.

Anytime I'm writing, I feel my Father's pleasure. Yet, it's more productive when I've prepared the spiritual atmosphere. It is true of any gifting I have been given; raising children, gardening, working jobs or businesses, playing musical instruments and even maintaining a home. I want Abba to be involved in everything I do, and Abba wants to be involved, as well.

If you are purpose driven, being alone in secret places with

Papa God has research and development keys for using who we are to accomplish the things we do. He is also a creative strategist. And with patience and quietness we will be sure to hear all his important details.

Most importantly, and frequently lesser prioritized, is the simplicity of being alone with God. Joshua was an example of a heart desiring to know Yahweh. He learned from Moses the importance of being face to face with him. It's where he learned dependence on his presence and obedience to his direction. By extension of his convictions and leadership, he stirred up the faith of those around him.

Being his dwelling place and not mere objects of obedience to his administration, he is our secret habitation of mutual love. From that Tent of Meeting, we live and function and have our identity.[i] How much more we need this understanding when unlocking the Golden Scroll. Without intimacy, the power of revelation and transformation from the Word is weakened. We need our secret places.

Where, when and what are your secret places? You may have one or several. When may be as important as where and what. Where may be that place that is like no other. These are places you experience God.

My alarm goes off at the same time every weekday morning. It is rare to be awakened by it, though. I'm usually awake before its set time. Why? Frequently, Papa starts talking before I'm awake. I hear his voice and my mind has no clutter to dull what he's saying. Sometimes he's waiting for me, and I simply know it. At other *when* moments, I've had enough sleep and I get up to be with him, wait for him and pray for people and things that come to mind.

A picture of this solitude is one of me leaning against the door frame of a cabin gazing down an open plain toward majestic mountains; reminiscent of years we lived in the Rocky Mountains. I'm listening for more of his voice and pondering what he has already said. There's no sense of urgency until he says there is.

My wife experiences an open door with God in her garden; a *where* place. Listening is a pleasure there. God gives birth and grows stuff, so does my wife; she's an intercessor and gardener. They have a oneness in their garden that touches her like no other.

Reading the bible for the simple purpose of fulfilling a daily task may leave us feeling there should be something more substantial for our commitment of time. After all, it is the *living* Word and we expect a *connection* with its inner being. But sometimes it doesn't happen. We've all had those experiences. When reading is our goal, we often think about the reading task. Its orientation is clouding the atmosphere and we want the job completed so we can check it off our list for the day. It's an easy distraction from internalizing what we read and gaining the Word's life-giving output[ii] and making it food for our Spirit.

I'm not saying a daily read or listen plan is wrong in any fashion. It's staple bread of life. But if we want a living feast, we need quality time and a skill-set for finding the best ingredients. To convert this food model to heart-changing treasure, interdependent keys unlock the Word's brilliance.

Unlocking the Golden Scroll is both a methodic scripture workout and an intuitive discovery of their mysteries. It is intentionally simple in design, with headroom to maximize picture building capability. With practice and with Holy Spirit's help, these keys unlock the Golden Scroll; the living Word of God; and infuse who we are with its contents.

With one key presented above, the following briefly describe other keys.

Key two involves taking apart the scripture to be studied. It involves highlighting key words and phrases, followed with deeper digging in English analysis and historical usage. Many English translations use words commonly used elsewhere (i.e.—the UK or Australia) or formerly used in the past but not in current colloquial practice. When we hear or read these words, their fullness doesn't register. We often read through them without impact on our understanding. When we catch the shortfall of comprehension, it's time to stop and explore.

Exploring original languages; key three; reveal extended design. Why is that? Hebrew and Greek are powerful and uniquely pictorial languages. English is a hybrid of several languages; ancient and modern; and often technical. It's constantly changing and doesn't reveal all of what needs to be said to make a full connection with the words.

As I have said before, Scripture has layers. It's not unusual to find a spiritual reality or truth one time and be surprised later to understand it was just one piece of a greater picture. Theology and doctrine have often stayed at one piece and not built other pieces together for the full blessing of truth activated by faith. I'm not saying theology and doctrine are unimportant in any way. What I am bringing to this table is the idea we have yet to see and believe all God wants to reveal. I said it in the last chapter as well. And when he reveals, he wants us to receive and respond. As we continue to respond, he wants to activate and use his revelations to grow us into his likeness and empower us to reach the lost.

One of my favorite keys is questions. A set of simple questions will get us started. Basic journalism questions include who, what, where, why, when and how. Using these to build deep-reaching queries from the texts we study produce far-reaching answers. A well-crafted question will take us to new and exciting places.

Observations and deductions; our investigative connections

117

keys. These keys improve with use and training; like exercise and practice. This is the core which develops seeing. Over time, your discernment levels to observe and deduct increase.

Observance of words, phrases and incidents is the power of discovering interesting and important gems. After observing answers and looking at them again, deductions can be made. This process develops more questions. Run with it until this process is satisfied.

I like mysteries and I have read everything of Sherlock Holmes. A statement he spoke several times had an impact on my way of doing things. He would tell a prospective client, "Start at the beginning and tell me everything. I want to hear every detail no matter how insignificant you may think it to be." His point was, his clients often brushed aside details, devaluating their worth. To him every detail was important until it wasn't. They were significant to his elements of observation. Even when observations and deductions threads ended without result, something it *wasn't* was revealed as well.

Deduction has simple structures: if ... then, cause ... effect, what's revealed ... what's hiding ... mysterious stuff it seems. But, when accomplished with the Holy Spirit present, it's fun and enlightening.

Prayer, meditation and application; our intimate connections keys. Studying from the glory is the practice of listening for

Holy Spirit's voice while connected with the Word. He is the one who leads and teaches about truth while I search for it.

I often focus on one segment of scripture for days or even weeks. Once, I spent thirty days on Psalm 37. Something stands out one day and another thing the next. I learned to appreciate that my moods and mindsets change from day to day. These changes influence my encounters and observations with the Word. Consequently, what was hidden on day one is now revealed on another day. What influenced me yesterday may not influence what I see today.

Moreover, repeated and rephrased questions influence revelation Holy Spirit is giving. Today's snapshot adds to yesterday's and tomorrow's snapshots. The pieces form larger pictures and after a week or two I have an amazing canvas of a life-giving Wordscape; a mural which brings application and transformation.

The word *grammar* is either tainted or enhanced by the experiences of our earliest school years. In the larger scheme of things, grammar may seem irrelevant, hard to figure and boring. Most people think little about it as busy adults carrying on daily career and family life.

As treasure hunters of the Word, we should be aware of a few things; particularly when working with original Hebrew and Greek languages. These languages carry time, sequence and contrast markers in their grammar structures. English does not. These markers are clues.

I make a practice of comparing original language verbs and nouns. Nouns are persons, places or things. Verbs are actions. Associating one with the other enlarges the scope of definition, filling deeds with voice, tense and mood.

Search out matters like a wise king. Sleuth out mysteries. Pursue rabbit trails. Never buy into the idea there's nothing more to be discovered; there always is.

Footnotes:

i  Acts 17:28

ii  Hebrews 4:12 (any version)

# Pondering

*"We need silence to be alone with God, to speak to him, to listen to him, to ponder his words deep in our hearts. We need to be alone with God in silence to be renewed and transformed. Silence gives us a new outlook on life. In it we are filled with the energy of God himself that makes us do all things with joy." (Mother Teresa)*

Once upon a time in a backyard garden, lived several figurines nestled among shrubs and flowers. These small statuettes were my mother's interpretive expressions of her children's inner world. After her passing some years ago, I had the freedom to take the one about myself home and put it in my garden as a remembrance of what she thought of me.

Mom's depiction of my peculiar quirks looks like a huckleberry character from Mark Twain's imagination. The boy sits on a tree stump, his feet bare and a twig of wheat grass in his mouth. The droopy straw hat and frayed high-water overalls adds to his simplicity. He's bent over with one elbow on his knee and the knuckles of one hand under his chin, watching purposefully. The other hand holds a fishing pole draped across his lap with its hook unprepared for casting. His thoughts are not about fishing at all, but far away contemplating a creative something. I think Mom pegged it.

I keep this memento to remind myself of what I should be doing — pondering things. So, allow me to stand up and take my hat off, lay aside the fishing pole, and share my thoughts about pondering. Now if you will, take my seat at the stump and listen a while.

In case you're wondering, it's also called ruminating (chewing the cud), mulling it over and a dozen other things. So you may already have an idea what I'm talking about.

Pondering is different than the secret place you read about in the last chapter. Pondering is done anywhere and everywhere. It can be intentional or inspirational. A ponder can start in a noisy crowd and end in the quietness of a drive in the country. It's thinkifying about broad imaginative puzzlers or linear contemplators or whatever mindful. It's the freedom to openly consider a thing to simply see what's there and what could be there. It's an adventure in the vast expanse of processing things. And as often as it should, the end result of pondering should find a quiet place to be alone and have another ponder while looking like you're fishing.

I'm a creative. I write stories and novels when I'm not writing teachings like this. Ideas and their parts bloom from a single inspiring word, complete sentence, an afternoon's conversation or a week of people-watching. Mulling over stuff considers variables in a storyline and grows with endless turns, twists and tumbles. It's the funnerest part of creating.

But in the more serious sphere of biblical writing, scriptures don't always fit the framework of straight-up study. They need to be pondered, because they will carry the weight of advice, encouragement, advancement, and perhaps revelation for those that read it. These scriptures speak with relevance to existing situations or prepare us for what we are about to face. Pondering allows scripture to find its current heart-target. They must be considered with integrity.

On other occasions scripture appears to lack depth of understanding. An example of this is emotion the written Word often lacks; it feels stiff. One must read between the lines to find Father's character. In doing so, emotion can be envisioned. What happens with me, contemplation; another word for pondering; provokes a short story which creates a fictional context with overlaid emotional expressions. These stories help me grasp important truths through Father's eyes.

Initially, having read a portion of the Word, I ponder what

is there. Perhaps it may be explained as lingering or hovering over the words, watching for something to come alive. Or, my ponderings may key on one or more of the unlocking processes written in the chapters which follow. By-the-way, the results of using the unlocking keys in the next chapters should have their moments of ponderance also.

One thought before moving on. A companion asset to pondering is journaling; written or electronic. If you already journal, a separate bible study journal will simplify finding previous thoughts that link with current ones. It will also provide space for test-running expanded ideas and forming questions.

# Ask Questions

*Statements create debate*
*Stories unlock hearts*
*Questions open minds*

Reflecting on Jesus' communication styles, he made statements and stimulated passionate disputes. He created stories and unlocked new revelation; some understood while others did not. His questions often stirred offence where hearts were immovably hard. At other times, his questions caused consideration about what they believed and why. For good or ill, his means of contact had impact.

One example is the biblical story of the prodigal son; which isn't just about one son. It's about three people with different hearts being a family doing life together. The sons in the story had important questions revealing different points.[i] Without questions, would the points have been made? Aha! My question provoked you to think about reading the story to see what I'm talking about. You can do that later, here's the questions.

Younger son: "Father, don't you think it's time to give me the share of your estate that belongs to me?"

Older son: "Father, listen! How many years have I been working like a slave for you, performing every duty you've asked as a faithful son?"

While the questions highlight each son's dysfunction, the chief point is the father's grace toward both.

To the younger son: "Son, you're home now." The end result was a high celebration.

To the older son: "My son, you are always with me by my side. Everything I have is yours to enjoy."[ii] The father's correction was equally gracious. He pointed out that welcoming the lost son home was the important issue at hand. The other son saw what he didn't have and lost touch with what he did have; apparently working hard for what he already had.

The parable of the lost sheep reinforces Jesus' heart about the lost: "In the same way, there will be a glorious celebration in heaven over the rescue of one lost sinner who repents, comes back home, and returns to the fold — more so than all the righteous people who never strayed away."[iii]

Many good sermons expand further on the prodigal, the father's heart and the other son of course. But I'm using the text as an example of questions and what they stir up. Questions create receptors in our minds that answers fill.

If one desires to create a dialogue, make a statement, ask a question or tell a story. Jesus made observational assertions designed to change how his disciples viewed life and provoked them to ask questions. Sometimes their questions stayed among each other. Sometimes they were so baffled, the questions couldn't be formed. But Jesus knew and often answered what was in their hearts.

An encounter with a rich man astonished the disciples. Jesus said at that time how difficult it was for the rich to enter God's kingdom realm.[iv] Those who heard what he said asked, "Who then can be saved?"

Questions turn on searches for raw materials to build and shape new thought structures or create building pieces. As pieces join together, they reform structures or construct more detailed and bigger pictures.

Questions with yes or no answers often have little value. You can answer a yes/no question in your head to set up carefully crafted questions on paper or computer. But it should always be followed with another question; such as, If so . . ., Given that . . ., What then . . .?

Crafted questions drill down to hidden treasure. When

127

practiced, they produce results worth the investment of time and effort. They will deepen daily conversations, transform your inner life and create hunger for more.

I love taking crafted questions off the page and inserting them in conversations and bible studies. I appreciate perspectives not my own. What other people share provoke me to take another step into the spiritual reality I'm seeking to own.

As stated before, basic journalism has six buildable basics: who, what, when, where, how and why. These basics focus on specific targets and stimulate fruitful next-step queries.

Here are a few examples of basic questions: "What are the key words and key phrases in this sentence or paragraph?" "Why was that said?" "How does that relate to faith, hope and love?" "Where is God in the middle of this?"

Look for repetition and progression, contrast and comparison, cause and effect, written explanations revealing motivation. Wherever I see the word mystery, I look for anything biblical which sheds light on it. Next-step questions would be: "Where have I seen this before?" or "Has this been stated elsewhere?"

Jesus said abstract things that left my linear thinking missing the point he was trying to make. Luke 17:1-10 is a conversation between Jesus and his disciples that jumps the rails and goes in another direction — more than once. We do it often in daily chats; we adjust and keep going. But to see it in scripture is a fun challenge.

In the first paragraph Jesus talks about betrayal, punishment, accountability, repentance and forgiveness. Not too hard, straight up relationship tools. But the disciples respond with, "Lord, you must increase our measure of faith!" My response: "WHAT? That doesn't fit!" Whereupon, Jesus responds about authentic faith and moving obstructions. But Jesus didn't wait for a response and quickly left off to pick up with the heart of a servant. My response? This doesn't follow sequential logic.

I shifted my questioning to focus on the white space between the lines and use deduction and observation to form more questions. "Is there a single point in common here?" "If so, why is it not obvious?" "What is the Father's heart if he were involved?" "What character or attitude would he want from me if I were involved?"

Now, this is where I slip in the idea that God will be involved with the answers to your questions. After all, it's his Word and you are his and he's in you. A real-life situation was about to answer one or more of my questions about this passage. My wife, Ann, fell and sprained her ankle. God used her pain to answer the attitude question about me and the heart question about him. To keep this chapter from being unduly long, the story is included as a Real-Life chapter to read at your convenience.

My point is to be ready for answers to your questions. They may be presented in real situations. If the question is important to you, it's important to God.

Moving along with potential questions regarding the Luke 17 passage.

How does one objective hinder the other? What are the strengths and weaknesses of each? Where does each idea take me? Why do I need to be aware? If at least one of these is a strategic question that will unlock a beautiful understanding, it is worth pursuing.

If you find yourself on a rabbit trail, be thoughtful about returning to your original path of thought. Some of my greatest riches are found when I'm not looking for them.

With building blocks presented and freedom to be curious, you're set up for good question crafting. It's the research and development lab from which scripture studies are put to the test and proven to be useful. Some application questions would be, "If what is here before me is true, how would I be different if I truly believed it? What would my life be like if I owned it whole-heartedly? What in my spirit could possibly be transformed and made powerful?" No doubt, you will discover more.

My analytics with questions are simple. Ask questions, get answers, then make deductions and observations and form another set of questions if needed. After all the years, I go to them without thinking. But your mind will function different than mine (that's probably good). Be adventurous and explore; discover the excitement of finding treasure with questions, deductions[v] and observations.[vi]

Questions open minds. I have no idea who made those original statements at the beginning of this chapter.[vii] It's true, though. Questions get us looking in places we might not inherently go and digging for ideas hidden outside the fringes of our current perspectives.

Seeking, asking and knocking may not be all about questions. Certainly, it is part of it and includes the curiosity of a seeker. Large or small, the Lord delights in every step we make toward him. If we are not finding what we are seeking, perhaps our questions need attention.

There are two words to close this chapter; subjective and objective. Subjective is the influence of personal feelings, tastes or opinions. Objective is the influence of unbiased data or phenomena. Since we are dealing with unseen spiritual realities in addition to tangible principles of biblical truth, it is important that we know the difference and use them wisely.

And so, there are mysteries to unpack and practical solutions that need revealing — if we pursue them. And if in our pursuit, we are given answers, let us be good stewards of the treasure we are given. When our King causes us to have eyes to see and ears to hear, it is to our honor he is trusting us with riches of his Kingdom.

*"Things never discovered or heard of before, things beyond our ability to imagine — these are the many things God has in store for all his lovers. But God now unveils these profound realities to us by the Spirit. Yes, he has revealed to us his inmost heart and deepest mysteries through the Holy Spirit, who constantly explores all things." (1 Corinthians 2:9-10)*

*"Lord, you are great and worthy of the highest praise! For there is no end to the discovery of the greatness that surrounds you. Generation after generation will declare more of your greatness and declare more of your glory." (Psalm 145:3-4)*

May we be faithful with what we are given.

Footnotes:

i In some translations, the questions are formed as statements.

ii Read John 17

iii Luke 15:4-7, Matthew 18:12-14, The parable of the lost coin also makes this statement.

iv Matthew 19:16-26, Mark 10:17-31, Luke 18:18-30

v Deduction is the process of reasoning in which a conclusion follows from the stated premise; inference by reasoning from the general to the specific. It is a systematic method of deriving conclusions that cannot be false when the premises are true.

vi Observation is the act or instance of noticing, perceiving, regarding attentively or watching; after which a statement is made.

vii I heard it for the first time from Aaron Tesauro. Kingdom Culture Conference, June 2019. (Bethel Church, Redding)

# What is English?

Let's say you've asked someone for their understanding of what a word means, and their response is, "Look it up in the dictionary." Where do you go from there? It's the future and something in print is scarce.

Kaleb goes to the garage and punches in a code to a hermetic locker. A whoosh of air and the whine of hydraulics opens the door. He walks into the small room and lights click on. A table in front of him has a single item. With more than average effort, Kaleb lifts the thick Carrara marble cover and swings it gently to one side. Lamb-skin pages lay before him. And with eyes of wonder for knowledge, Kaleb touches the pages as if they were sacred. He's grateful he learned the ancient script.

I want to tell Kaleb, "I've got an e-dictionary right here on my phone. And it weighs less than the eighty-pound wounder displayed on your desk." He can't hear me, though, he's in another world. For many people, language and grammar (whether English or otherwise) is an unknown world. But, it isn't difficult to understand.

Like many modern languages, English is influenced by globalization; it always has been. According to Britannica.com, "English belongs to the Indo-European family of languages and is therefore related to most other languages spoken in Europe and western Asia." In other words, it's a hybridized and adoptive language with more than 300 ethnic influencers spanning nearly two thousand years.

Familiar (also called colloquial) expressions of English words have different meanings than formal expressions of the same word. Also, definitions change at the whims of one generation after another.[i]

Why should this be important to know? In a word, this is about *trust*. Allow me to shake your trust of what you use as the best meanings and discover the *depth* of meanings revealed in a good dictionary and how those words were used throughout English-speaking history.[ii] This practice will guard you from drawing under-researched and powerless conclusions.

With that understood, let's simplify the English definition focus. Our pursuit is having the Word of God (the bible, the Golden Scroll) living in us richly (in abundance, generously).[iii] So, we want our explorations and findings to be plentiful, even if some of it is unusable.

Can we admit there are words in the English scriptures we don't ordinarily use? Of course. Yet, reading words not part of our regular vocabulary weakens depth of impact. Our options are to assume we know or seek clarity. It may be short-sighted to believe the English we use every day is all we need and leave something wonderful undiscovered.

In addition to definitions there are synonyms. Synonyms have the same or nearly the same meaning as another word. Knowing synonyms with familiar meanings broaden the pictorial canvas of our language; a valuable key for unlocking the Golden Scroll.

To reinforce my purpose, lets investigate an example. One of my favorites is the word *redeem*. My dictionary has nine flavors.

One . . . to recover ownership of by paying a specified sum

Two . . . to pay off; like a promissory note.

Three . . . to turn in and receive something in exchange.

Four . . . to discharge or fulfill; like a pledge or promise.

Five . . . to convert into cash.

Six . . . to set free; rescue or ransom; to recover from captivity with a payment

Seven . . . to save from a state of sinfulness and its conse-quences.

Eight . . . to make amends for, to atone for, to offset a short-coming.

Nine . . . to restore the honor, worth, or reputation of.

Now, let's have a little fun overlaying all the above defini-tions with two similar scriptures.

"Walk in wisdom toward those who are outside, redeeming the time."[iv]

"See then that you walk circumspectly, not as fools but as wise, redeeming the time, because the days are evil."[v]

Here's an unexpected opportunity. *Circumspectly* is not a word I would hear in a normal conversation with my peers. What's your first impression? Now look it up in the dictionary and compare with your thoughts. Check the origins and see how it differs from the definition. It may reveal the original intent. Look for synonyms.

*Circumspect:*

Etymology: from late Middle English usage (1375-1425) and the Latin word circumspectus. Circum-, to take heed + specere, to look (spek in Indo-European roots). Definition: heedful of potential consequences, careful and sensible, watchful.

Synonyms: cautious, guarded, discreet, prudent, attentive.

Now read the passage again. Perhaps the etymology was of little help. But the definition and synonyms helped position what we needed to know precisely. Now I understand what is expected of me.

Fool is generally misunderstood when compared with street language. The dictionary meanings are quite broad in scope. Defining these and discovering their synonyms would be a bonus. You'd be surprised to find a fool is some kind of yummy dessert. Go figure.

Rabbit trails just pop up everywhere. Sometimes I give myself permission to take the bait and run. But getting back to the points of redemption.

As you see, each variation of the word *redeem* has a different setting. Yet, there is similar substance in each one. Now read the greater context of the scripture (the verses before and after), and do the same thing again with the nine definitions.

Having done this exercise, connect the definitions with the person and nature of Jesus as our redeemer. Ponder who he is in each definition and discover how wonderful the work of the cross and his resurrection are incorporated within redemption.

Since this is an exercise, I am quickly overreaching my

commitment to keeping this simple. But I'm showing the process and how it can be as focused or as free as you like. When you have plenty of time, enjoy the journey. Under pressure for results? Resist the rabbit trails.

In some cases, pursuing English definitions leaves us wanting more. When the English dictionary falls short of shedding significant light on the biblical context, there is potential in shifting to original languages for new keys. We will cover this in the next chapter.

Footnotes:

i Colloquial defined: Characteristic of or appropriate to the spoken language; informal and coversational. Relating to conversation; typical of ordinary or familiar language. Can have regional influences.

ii This is etymology: the origin and historical development of a linguistic form as shown by determining its basic elements, earliest known use, and changes in form and meaning, tracing its transmission from one language to another, identifying its cognates in other languages, and reconstructing its ancestral form where possible.

iii Colossians 3:16. Strong's #G4146

iv  Colossians 4:5, NKJV

v  Ephesians 5:16, NKJV

# There's no Language Like an Old Language

My academic and church life in the early eighties formed an on-ramp for where I am today with biblical languages. I lived in Southern California attending bible college and going to Church on the Way. Jack Hayford was the pastor and he was leading the congregation away from the King James Version of the bible and toward a newer translation. For a season, he publicly compared two recently published versions. I bought one of each and read both, cover-to-cover. It didn't take long to see they had problems with agreement. And that problem stirred my curiosity more than just a little.

Pursuing original languages seemed the only remedy to satisfy my curiosity. I committed a year to learning biblical Hebrew with the condition that if at the end of that year my why wasn't satisfied, I would not pursue it further. Before the year was done, though, I was hooked. A passion ignited in that short time which continues to this day.

I discovered how two English translations could disagree and remain within the scope of translating practices. The translators were compelled toward choices based on translation rules and shades of doctrinal belief. That is and was acceptable.

English cannot compare with the breadth and depth of Hebrew and Greek. Scholars A T Robertson and Kenneth Wuest reinforce this claim. Although these specialists are no longer around, their works certainly are. Quotes from introductions to their works reveal why they encourage my commitment to keep going.

Kenneth Wuest points out: *"When one has read all the various translations, each of which brings out some different shade of meaning from the inexhaustible richness of the Greek text, there still remains a large untranslatable wealth of truth to which only a Greek student has access. The reason for this is that in a translation which keeps to a minimum of words, that is, where one English word for instance, is the translation of one Greek word, it is impossible for the translator to bring out all the shades of meaning of the Greek word. It sometimes requires ten or a dozen words to give a well-rounded, full-orbed concept of the Greek word."*[i]

A T Robertson says it this way: *"I have called these volumes,*

*Word Pictures for the obvious reason that language was origi-nally purely pictographic.*

*"Words have never gotten wholly away from the picture stage. These old Greek words in the New Testament are rich with meaning. They speak to us out of the past and with lively images to those who have eyes to see. It is impossible to trans-late all of one language into another. Much can be carried over, but not all. Delicate shades of meaning defy the translator. But some of the very words of Jesus we have still as he said: "The words that I have spoken unto you are spirit and are life" (John 6:63). We must never forget that in dealing with the words of Jesus we are dealing with things that have life and breath."*[xii]

The words of Jesus have life and breath. Hebrews 4:12 and 13 support Robertson's statement; even expanding on it. The Word of God is living and active; a piercing sword separating soul and spirit; discerning considerations, musings and ways of thinking of the heart. It brings everything out of hiding with the purpose to transform and give life.

Time and again, original languages has carried me to places English could not go. And I have reaped rich treasure as my reward. I have seen Papa God's identity through these journeys and hope to have many more. I offer this part of the book as an invitation to start your expedition of treasure hunting God's Word whether you end up learning biblical languages or not.

Getting started is simple, and you establish the pace and level of study. At the entry level, it's much like finding definitions for English words. After the key words and phrases are singled out, find the Hebrew or Greek equivalent through concordances. There are websites for online access to these tools.

A concordance is an alphabetical index of all the words in a text, showing every contextual occurrence of a word. In this case, a biblical text according to the translation being used.

More detailed concordances are called lexicons. A lexicon is a dictionary with a specific subject, style and vocabulary; often including historical and extra-biblical usage. They have a deeper penetration of meaning and nuances. Intermediate levels require a simple knowledge of the Greek and Hebrew alphabets to maneuver through them.

Self-help workbooks; called primers; are a way to get traction with basic alphabets and grammar. Language history and how they have been written both ancient and modern is included.

When your desire for more is hard to satisfy, there are serious avenues of study. Forming a small group with people of mutual interests is incredibly fun and productive. It is also a good means for accountability with accuracy.

Many bible and secular colleges have online courses for Greek and Hebrew. You'll get straight up academic application without embellishments; which can be stuffy or fun depending on the instructor. Wherever possible, make this part of your journey fun.

Other non-academic courses are available which may also lead you to Hebrew roots and Jewish studies. My suggestion is keeping scripture studies the main thing as cultural studies can be a rather intoxicating rabbit hole. Simply remember our goal is to become like Jesus in every way. He is the perfect image we seek to identify with, not the law (torah).

Your journey with biblical languages will be unique to you, if you choose to make it. Every believer should engage it on some level if possible. The benefits are extraordinary and will present much substance for pondering.

Footnotes:

i  Wuest's Word Studies from the Greek New Testament

ii  Robertson's Word Pictures in the Greek New Testament

iii  Metamorphosis. Strong's Greek #3339 (Romans 12:2, 2 Corinthians 3;18)

iv  King James Version, New International Version, English Standard Version, New American Standard Bible, The Message, New Revised Standard Version and languages other than English. There are several online concordances with search tools. Check christianbook.com for resource sets and good pricing. Used versions abound for little money and can even be found at yard and estate sales.

# An Unlocking Experience

The keys presented in this book have potential. To unlock spiritual realities in the treasury of the Word of God takes practice. Making these keys fruitful will need persistence. When opportunities often show up unannounced or spontaneous conversations trigger a desire to go deeper, these tools will take you where you want to go at any time.

The following is an example of one I had and I will close with it. Its journey isn't linear and follows the meandering processes of a treasure hunter. Consequently, the conclusions don't always answer the questions. But they are conclusions nonetheless to feed the pondering mind.

An off-hand question during a conversation provoked doubt about my calling as a writer and especially storytelling. What was my motive? Is it a biblical calling? Does it require faith?

I considered the words Jesus used to explain points he

conveyed. They were parables; fictional stories with relevant application. But that was Jesus. How could I justify putting scripture, their principles and their revelations into story form as he did?

"As he is, so are we in this world," came to mind. It encouraged me to consider Jesus used fictive situations to convey spiritual realities and unlock hearts. So, I'm okay with doing the same. But, before I went any further along that line, I sought the context for the phrase. I found it in 1 John 4 using my New American Standard, which has Greek words and Strong's numbering under it.[i]

> "We have come to know and have believed the love which God has for us. God is love, and the one who abides in love abides in God, and God abides in him. By this, love is perfected with us, so that we may have confidence in the day of judgement; because as he is, so also are we in this world." (verses 16 & 17)[ii]

As love is perfected in us, we are as he is. Not as he was, but as he is. Further illumination is given in Colossians 3.

> Christ's resurrection is your resurrection too. This is why we are to yearn for all that is above, for that's where Christ sits enthroned at the place of all power, honor, and authority! Yes, feast on all the treasures of the heavenly realm and fill your

*thoughts with heavenly realities, and not with the*
*distractions of the natural realm.*

*Your crucifixion with Christ has severed the tie*
*to this life, and now your true life is hidden away in*
*God in Christ. And as Christ himself is seen for who*
*he really is, who you really are will also be revealed,*
*for you are now one with him in his glory! [ verses 1*
*through 4]*

With location and context satisfied, I continued to read.
When I came to 1 John 5:4, there was an emdash. Why the
emdash? It's not in the Greek text. It was a cue to me there
was trouble translating the Greek. It needed investigation. But
before I go on, here's the text (see also John 16:33).

*"For whatever is born of God overcomes the*
*world; and this is the victory that has overcome the*
*world — our faith." (NKJV)*

Using the Strong's numbering I checked out my Greek
dictionary.[iii] I looked at the noun form from the verse, then
extended my observations to the verb and adjective forms as
well to expand the overall picture. In every case, there was a
Hebrew cross-reference. I remembered several teachings I
heard that faith as we know it is not part of the Old Testament; it
is not mentioned as much as it is in the New Testament. If this is
true, then why the Hebrew cross-references? Off to the Hebrew

149

dictionary!<sup>iv</sup>

I understand this trail wanders a bit; be patient with my thinking processes.

A word search of the Old Testament produced one mention of faith in a positive statement. It was at the very end in Habakkuk; "But the just shall live by faith." All other references were about faithfulness. Most of those were in reference to acts which honored Yahweh. While others specified people who were faithful (Abraham, Moses, David, etc.).

Okay, not finding the results I'm looking for. What's another word for faith? Believe — do another search using believe. Yeah, now we're getting somewhere. Lots of references here. Now, check the Hebrew words used for both words — they're different. Or are they? Different usage, but same roots. Go back and check the Greek reference for faith. References match the believe search.

Observations: translators used faith in the New Testament but used believe in the Old Testament. Why did they do that? Answer: don't know yet. (Here's a guess: often times the oldest translations established a trend which was honored in modern translating. I'm seeing this trend being corrected.)

On the other hand, Jesus addressed the religious leaders as not believing what he said. But he addressed his disciples as having little faith. I see a picture in development here. Maybe believing is the presence of faith; even if it's a little. Is unbelief the absence of faith? Hmmmm.

Deductions: While faith was necessary even with observing the law, faithfulness in performance was a more predominant activity; even when it did not reflect the heart of God perfectly. The religious leaders were a case in point. Old Testament leaders created traditions around the law for appearances to justify something lacking in the heart.

What was lacking? They did not believe what came from the mouth of God. They created traditions to justify their unbelief and called it righteousness. In so doing, they locked themselves and the people to a ball and chain of self-righteousness and put a wall around the truth which separated them from their freedom.

Do I do things like that? Absolutely. Prayer: examine me, Lord. It would be easy to point to the faults of others and what they lack. Not my job. But what about my own heart? Let nothing be hidden that the truth may be alive in me.

I'm having fun exploring this vein. I've examined motive and found love. I've explored a little on faith and compared a little with faithfulness. I've gained important understanding while examining my own heart and discovered it takes the empowerment of love and trust to overcome negativity.

151

Conclusion: stay faithful to my calling as a writer and keep it motivated by love. If God has something else in mind, he'll let me know.

Although there is more to be explored and applied, but I'll leave it undone for now. Walking you through this short version of my processing gives you a snapshot of how these keys unlock the Golden Scroll for you. Since your thinking processes are uniquely gifted, you may have different results.

As I draw this second section as well as the book to a close, I understand I have merely given you appetizers to stimulate your appetite for more of the father, Jesus, his Word and the Spirit. It would be irresponsible to bring you here and leave you alone.

If you have questions or comments, there are two ways to contact us by email. One is through the publisher: (jimpowell@wanderingstream.org). The other is: (friends@creativestirrings.org).

May your journey on the path of life be blessed with riches.

*"You may have an abundance of wealth, piles of gold and jewels, but there is something of far greater worth: speaking revelation words of knowledge."* *(Proverbs 20:15)*

Footnotes:

i  I use a software that has several bible versions with this trait available. It also has Hebrew words in the Old Testament.

ii  Or "because we are what he is in this world." The verb tense is important. We are not like Jesus was, but because of grace, we are like he is now: pure and holy, seated in heaven, and glorified. See Rom. 8:30; Eph. 2:6; Col. 3:1–4. Faith has transferred his righteousness to us. [Footnote from The Passion Translation]

iii  Dictionary of Biblical Languages with Semantic Domains: Greek. James A Swanson

iv  Dictionary of Biblical languages with Semantic Domains: Hebrew. James A Swanson. There is also one for Aramaic.

Made in the USA
Middletown, DE
04 December 2025

24025214R00091